can't go wrong

coo

ORLAN

DAILY EXPRESS

SIMON & SCHUSTER
A VIACOM COMPANY

First published in Great Britain by
Simon & Schuster UK Ltd, 2002
A Viacom Company

1 3 5 7 9 10 8 6 4 2

Simon & Schuster UK Ltd
Africa House
64–78 Kingsway
London WC2B 6AH

Cover illustration by Louise Fairchild
Designed by Jane Humphrey
Typeset by Stylize Digital Artwork
Printed in Italy

A CIP catalogue record for this book is
available from the British Library

ISBN 0 743 20755 6

CONTENTS

FOREWORD

I have great respect and regard for Orlando Murrin, both as the editor of the BBC Good Food *magazine and for his lively daily Clever Cook column in the Daily Express. I am delighted he has compiled this new* Daily Express *cookbook, for it provides a permanent record of some of his favourite dishes.*

I always read Orlando's recipes with great interest, for there is something special about them. Maybe it appears that the recipe is for a dish I know, and have cooked a number of times, but generally there will be an unexpected twist that promises a different flavour. Sometimes the recipe is based upon a food that is new on the market and probably unknown to most people. This is where Orlando shows he is rightly called the 'Clever Cook', for he explains the value of the ingredient, its origin, where to obtain it, as well as its advantages. The explicit information means that people can look forward to creating a new and exciting dish – without any problems.

He is a very brave man to call his new book the Can't Go Wrong Cookbook, *for that is a challenging statement. However, knowing the careful testing that goes into all his recipes, I am sure the title is justified. If cooks follow his carefully worded instructions they will be sure of success.*

Now let me whet your appetites. On a chilly day, I shall make Orlando's Cream of Velvet Soup (page 16), for it includes a favourite vegetable of mine – parsnips. A kedgeree has been famous for generations but the recipe in the book (page 29) gives it a spicier flavour. Even if you have never skied, you will want to make the Après-Ski Supper (page 26), with its enticing mixture of bacon and cheese. Cornbread is popular at the present time and Orlando's special recipe (Golden Cornbread, page 176) shows how easy it is to prepare. Pork with Olives and Mahogany Roast Chicken (pages 100 and 99) make familiar foods enticing. Bête Noire (page 139) is a mysterious title – it disguises what Orlando Murrin describes as a 'Devilish Chocolate Cake'.

I am sure this book will be as popular as Orlando's first one, for it is full of practical and imaginative information with recipes that make you want to cook.

Marguerite Patten

For Peter

ACKNOWLEDGEMENTS

This book is a compilation of my own original recipes, recipes sent to me by Daily Express readers and ideas inspired by books, magazines, restaurants and other chefs. I would like to thank specifically – for recipes, inspiration, ideas or help in compiling the book – Aldo Zilli; Alex Mackay; Allegra McEvedy; Amy Willcock; Eric Treuillé; Fiona McCowan; Francesco Manzoli; Friends of Guys' and St Thomas' Hospitals; Gabriele Fyjis-Walker; Ghislaine Infield; Green Street Seafood Café; Joan Coleman and the ladies of the Vale of the White Horse; Joyce Yates; Kate Birk; Lesley Mackey; Lorna Wing; Margaret Fineran; Mary Cadogan and the BBC Good Food team; Michael Cox; Molly Parkin; Mrs Couzens; Pat Bradshaw; New Covent Garden Soups; Pat Steggall; Peter Steggall; Sarah Astell; Sarah Crockett; Sue Ashworth; Sue Lawrence; Susanna Gelmetti; Thane Prince; Victoria Lloyd-Davies; Vivien Jawett; Vivienne Coombe.

I am particularly grateful to my recipe tester, Patsy Murrin, and taste quality controller, Pat Murrin, for ensuring each and every one of these recipes qualifies as 'can't-go-wrong'.

I would like to thank my loyal assistant Sarah Astell for her everlasting patience and good humour.

Finally, my thanks to my editing and publishing team. Sue McGeever, who commissioned the book, and Jocelyn Sizer and Bronwen Holly who work on the newspaper, and whose powers of observation and stamina I find marvellous. And at Simon and Schuster, my inestimable editors Anna Hitchin and Susanna Clarke.

INTRODUCTION

Do you believe life is too short to skin a pepper? Are you bored with beautiful pictures that don't look anything like the recipe when it comes out of the oven? Do you blame yourself when a recipe goes wrong, thinking you must have set the timer wrongly, or mis-measured — because after all, the recipe is bound to be right? This book is dedicated to every cook who wants a decent result every single time they step into the kitchen. I happen to think that, if you enjoy cooking, this is what you deserve.

Having tried out literally thousands of recipes over the years, I am aware of the rollercoaster ride offered by most recipes published in newspapers, magazines and books. Even within the same cookbook you can find superb recipes and out-and-out catastrophes. Here, tried and tested, is my own personal selection of favourite recipes, all of them given their début in the Daily Express. They work for me and I sincerely believe they will work for you.

Many of the dishes you'll find within are adaptations of recipes old and new. There aren't, in truth, many food combinations still waiting to be discovered — someone, somewhere is bound to have got there first. But it's what you do with those particular ingredients that makes a dish special.

I've learnt so much over the years about customising dishes to make them my own, and I have a few golden rules. When making a recipe for the first time, I follow it scrupulously. If nothing else you'll find out whether it's been properly tested by the writer, which is useful knowledge for the future. I follow this advice even if the recipe seems wrong. Only recently, I was making a dessert from a new book. The recipe didn't make any sense till about halfway through, when I suddenly realised it was one of those desserts which settles into a layer of sauce with a layer of sponge on top. If I'd started to adapt it halfway through I would have ended up with porridge.

Baking, in particular, is a bit like a chemistry experiment – all the components need to be added in the right proportion and in the right order. Once you know how a dish works, though, you can be as fancy-free as you wish.

I hope you will enjoy making the recipes in this book as much as I have. As ever, I have tried to make the cooking as straightforward and frill-free as possible, at the same time remembering that cooking is a pleasure, so you don't want it to be over before you've even started!

chapter 1

EASY SNACKS AND STARTERS

Modern life has gravitated away from three meals to a day to a more flexible approach, and even nutritionists now advise us to eat smaller meals more often. The recipes in this chapter are like a halfway house; some will make a light lunch, others an easy supper when you don't feel like cooking. If you take a fancy to one you can even serve it as a first course to a grander meal.

Most of these recipes can also be adapted down or up in size. Although many people worry about doing this, it isn't hard to get your head around if you use common sense as your guide. Cooking times usually remain about the same whether you halve or double a dish, and amounts of liquid judged by eye. When I was a beginner I used to find myself adding half an egg, but now I am more inclined to add just the yolk!

SWEET POTATO SOUP

I first discovered this recipe in a French magazine; the French are generally rather sniffy when it comes to exotic vegetables (they think sweetcorn and swede are fit only for cattle) – so it must be good. It is a lovely warm pink-gold colour and the flavour is exceptional. It is also low in fat, needing just a touch of crème fraîche, on account of the natural silky texture of the sweet potatoes.

EASY: *20 minutes to prepare, 30 minutes to cook; freezes well*

SERVES 10 – 12

1.2 litres/2 pints stock	**2 large onions, chopped roughly**
2 star anise, or ½ tsp five-spice powder	**1 head of celery, trimmed and sliced**
	salt and pepper
50 g/2 oz butter	To serve (optional):
2 large sweet potatoes, peeled and cut in chunks	**a little crème fraîche**
	snipped fresh chives

❶ Bring the stock to the boil with the star anise or five-spice powder and keep hot.

❷ Heat the butter in a large pan. Add the sweet potatoes and the onions and brown lightly – about 10 minutes. Add the celery and the stock and simmer for 30 minutes, till all is tender.

❸ Liquidise and then thin slightly with water, if necessary. Serve hot or cold, with a little crème fraîche and snipped chives – check the seasoning before serving.

TIP 🥣 If you haven't experienced sweet potatoes, try them baked in their jackets, just the way you would regular potatoes but for 15 minutes less time. Do not eat the skin, but be lavish with pepper and butter.

ROASTED TOMATO SOUP

I have long loved canned tomatoes; they are completely natural, have a beautiful colour and a lovely sweet, juicy flavour – and they're very convenient indeed. I would far rather use these during the winter months than those pallid tomatoes we import from southern Europe and North Africa, which are rock hard and taste sour.

NO TROUBLE: *10 minutes to prepare, 1 hour to cook; freezes well*

SERVES 8

2 × 400 g cans of plum tomatoes in natural juice

1 tbsp dark brown or muscovado sugar

25 g/1 oz butter

2 shallots or one small onion, chopped finely

2 tsp tomato purée

a pinch of ground allspice

1 tbsp plain flour

900 ml/1½ pints chicken or vegetable stock

3 tbsp double cream

1 tbsp brandy

salt and cayenne pepper

❶ Preheat the oven to 220°C/200°C fan oven/Gas Mark 7. Line a swiss-roll tin or baking tray with a lip with foil. Tip the tomatoes into a sieve set over a bowl to catch the juices. One by one, pick out the tomatoes and halve lengthways; use your fingers to remove most of the seeds and as much liquid as possible and lay on the baking sheet. Sprinkle with the sugar and roast for 30–40 minutes, till dry and beginning to singe at the edges. Allow to cool and carefully transfer to a bowl.

❷ Take a medium-size saucepan and heat the butter till foaming. Fry the shallots or onion with the tomato purée and allspice for 7–10 minutes, till softened. Add the flour and cook for 30 seconds; then, whisking constantly, gradually add the stock, tomato juices and tomatoes. Cover and simmer for 10 minutes.

❸ Liquidise (this will give a smoother result than a food processor). Then reheat with the cream. Add the brandy just before serving, and season to taste (if you have used stock cubes, do this with care as they are often rather salty).

AVGOLEMONO (EGG AND LEMON SOUP)

This marvellous Greek soup is no trouble and tastes quite fresh and wonderful. If you have the leftovers from a roast chicken in the fridge (or freezer), they are a good excuse to make it.

EASY: *allow 30 minutes (not including making stock)*

SERVES 6–8

2.25 litres/4 pints chicken stock
   (preferably home-made)
125 g/4 oz long-grain white rice
1 bay leaf
4 green cardamom pods, crushed,
   or 2 whole cloves
zest of 1½ medium lemons, pared
   off thinly with potato peeler

1½ tsp salt
2 large eggs, plus 2 yolks
50 ml/2 fl oz juice from the lemons
To garnish (optional):
1 large spring onion, sliced thinly
3 tbsp chopped fresh mint leaves

❶ Bring the stock to the boil in a medium pan. Add the rice, bay leaf, spices, zest and salt. Simmer till the rice is tender and the soup smells deliciously fragrant – about 20 minutes.

❷ Fish out the bay leaf, spices and zest and discard. Bring back to the boil.

❸ Whisk the eggs, yolks and lemon juice in a large bowl. Still whisking, slowly add about 425 ml/¾ pint of the hot stock – whisk until combined. Now pour the egg-stock mixture back into the pan and cook over low heat, stirring without cease, until the soup is slightly thickened and the odd wisp of steam appears – about 4–5 minutes. Do not boil. Divide between bowls, garnish, if you want, and serve at once.

BROCCOLI AND LIME SOUP

One of the best things about modern convenience foods is the brilliant fresh soups you can buy from the chiller cabinet. Now canned soup has its place – how could you beat Heinz tomato or cream of mushroom? – but the fresh soups in cartons or pouches, made with fresh seasonal ingredients, are almost as good as home-made.

One of the best brands is the New Covent Garden Soup Company and this recipe is an adaptation of one of their recipes.

EASY: *allow 1 hour; freezes well*

SERVES 4

a knob of butter	300 g/10 oz broccoli, divided
1 small onion, chopped	into florets
125 g/4 oz potatoes, peeled and	2 tbsp double cream
cubed	2 tsp creamed horseradish
900 ml/1½ pints vegetable or	salt and pepper
chicken stock	chopped fresh herbs, plus extra
juice and grated zest of 1 lime	to garnish

❶ Melt the butter and sweat the onion and potato gently for 5 minutes without colouring (see Tip). Add the stock, lime zest and juice. Cover and simmer for 15 minutes, till the vegetables are tender.

❷ Meanwhile, cook the broccoli till just tender, 5–10 minutes only. Set aside.

❸ Liquidise the potato mixture and then add the broccoli and liquidise again – but don't overprocess as you want the broccoli to remain quite chunky.

❹ Return to the pan and add the cream, horseradish and herbs. Check the seasoning – it needs plenty – and serve garnished with extra herbs.

TIP 'Sweating' is the process of gently cooking vegetables in fat. You can do it with the lid on or off, but keep the heat very moderate to prevent sticking, and shake or turn the pan frequently.

BRUSSELS SPROUT SOUP

Some people love making soup, others just aren't interested. But there is nothing more rewarding, and the pleasure stretches out over two or three days if you make a big batch.

EASY: *30 minutes to make, 40 minutes to cook; freezes well*

SERVES 8–10

1 tbsp oil

2 bacon rashers, rinded and chopped

1 onion, chopped

1 garlic clove, crushed

500 g/1 lb brussels sprouts,
   trimmed and halved

500 g/1 lb potatoes, peeled and sliced

1.2 litres/2 pints stock, vegetable
   water or mixture of water and
   cider or dry white wine

450 ml/¾ pint milk

grated nutmeg, salt and pepper

a knob of butter

3–4 tbsp cream, to serve

❶ Heat the oil and fry the bacon and onion for about 8 minutes till golden. Add the garlic for the last minute.

❷ Add the sprouts, potatoes and stock and cook, covered, till all is tender – 25–30 minutes.

❸ Liquidise and reheat with the milk. Season well with salt, pepper and nutmeg. Just before serving, stir in the knob of butter, which gives the soup a luxuriant extra depth. Put a swirl of cream in each dish.

TIP 🥄 You can make lovely crisp Stilton wafers to go with this. Preheat the grill and crumble 150 g/5 oz of Stilton cheese with 2 tbsp of fresh white breadcrumbs and 25 g/1 oz of finely chopped walnuts. Line a baking sheet with baking parchment and put the mixture in eight piles on it, well apart (use two sheets if too big to fit under the grill in one go). Grill for 1–2 minutes, till melted. Let cool and then transfer to a wire rack.

BUTTERNUT SQUASH SOUP
& CURRIED HORSERADISH

*I discovered this soup in Ludlow on my first visit to the food festival,
a mecca for food-lovers from all over the country. As well as being
exceptionally pretty, Ludlow boasts more Michelin-starred restaurants
per capita than anywhere else in Britain except London. The reason?
Gifted restaurateurs, fine local produce and the support of the local
population. This soup was invented by local cook Lesley Mackey.*
EASY: *allow an hour and a bit*

SERVES 6

1 butternut squash, about 625 g/1¼ lb	150 ml/¼ pint apple juice
1 cooking apple	salt and pepper
25 g/1 oz butter	a pinch of curry powder, to serve
1 onion, chopped finely	For the curried horseradish cream:
1–2 tsp curry powder	4 tbsp double cream
900 ml/1½ pints chicken or	2 tsp creamed horseradish
vegetable stock	½ tsp curry powder
1 tsp chopped fresh sage	

❶ Peel the squash, remove the seeds and chop the flesh. Peel, core and chop the apple.

❷ Heat the butter, add the onion and cook till soft. Stir in the curry powder and cook for 2 minutes, to bring out the flavour.

❸ Add the stock, squash, apple and sage. Bring to the boil, cover and simmer for 20 minutes till the vegetables are soft.

❹ Meanwhile, make the horseradish cream. Whip the cream and then stir in the horseradish and curry powder. Refrigerate till needed.

❺ When the soup is cooked, liquidise. Return to the pan, add the apple juice and season. Heat gently, without boiling.

❻ Serve each portion topped with a spoonful of the horseradish cream and a dusting of curry powder.

CREAM OF VELVET SOUP

I love caraway seeds but I appreciate not everyone does; leave them out, or substitute another slightly unusual spice such as juniper, or ground cumin.
EASY: *30 minutes to prepare, a good hour to cook (quicker if you cut the vegetables smaller); can be frozen at end of step 2*

SERVES 6 – 8

2 onions	600 ml/1 pint stock
1 parsnip	600 ml/1 pint milk or cider
1 turnip	a pinch of sugar
½ medium swede (about 500 g/1 lb	a splash of Worcestershire sauce
peeled weight)	salt and pepper
1 medium potato	For the welsh rarebit topping (optional):
4 celery sticks	1 slice of bread per person
2 garlic cloves	butter
25 g/1 oz butter	mustard
1 tbsp caraway seeds (optional)	25 g/1 oz grated cheese per person

❶ Peel the onions, parsnip, turnip, swede and potato. Wash and trim the celery. Slice all very finely – it is well worth getting out your food processor slicing disc for this quantity. Peel and finely chop the garlic.

❷ In a large, lidded pan, melt the butter. Add all the vegetables, cover and sweat for 15 minutes over a moderate heat, stirring periodically. Crush the caraway seeds in a pestle and mortar vigorously so that you have a powdery mixture (but some seeds will still be whole) and stir in, with the stock. Bring to a simmer and cook, covered, for 30–40 minutes.

❸ Liquidise in batches.

❹ Reheat, with the milk or cider, and season well with salt, pepper, a pinch of sugar and a splash of Worcestershire sauce.

❺ If serving with the topping, heat the grill. Toast the bread well on one side, turn over and lightly toast the other side. Cut into triangles. Now spread lightly with butter and mustard, sprinkle with the cheese and grill till melting. Transfer to heated soup bowls and ladle the soup round.

easy snacks and starters

16

BEST-EVER DEVILLED EGGS

My first-ever cookbook was Marguerite Patten's Everyday Cooking *and it was from this that, when I was about 20, I put together, rather clumsily, I dare say, but to great praise from everyone who tasted it, my first home-made egg mayonnaise. It is a dish fit for a king. More sophisticated, and perfect for a picnic, is this easy recipe.*

EASY: *allow 45 minutes*

SERVES 6

7 large free-range eggs, cold

3–4 tsp grainy mustard

3 tbsp mayonnaise, bought or home-made

1½ tsp cider vinegar

¼ tsp Worcestershire Sauce

salt and pepper

paprika, to garnish

❶ Put the eggs in a saucepan, cover with 2.5 cm/1 inch of water and bring to the boil over a high heat. Remove the pan from the heat, cover and let stand for 10 minutes. Meanwhile, fill a large bowl with cold water and lots of ice cubes.

❷ Transfer the eggs to the bowl and leave to cool for 5 minutes. This seems like a palaver but is the way to get gently set, non-rubbery egg whites and melt-in-the-mouth yolks.

❸ Now peel the eggs and slice each in half lengthways. Remove the yolks to a small bowl. Pick out the two scruffiest egg white halves and give them to the dog as an unexpected – though I am sure not undeserved – bonus. Arrange the remaining 12 egg white halves on a serving plate (you serve two egg-halves each).

❹ Mash the yolks with the remaining ingredients and salt and pepper to taste, till smooth. Ideally, pipe the mixture into the egg-white halves with a large star nozzle, mounding it above the surface; otherwise, spoon in neatly with a dessertspoon. A dusting of paprika is traditional in the Murrin family and looks good.

FLUFFY CHEESE RAMEKINS

This is an easy first course that I have been eating for as long as I remember, it being one of my mother's dinner-party dishes when I was growing up. I have a feeling that, in the sixties and seventies, attitudes to entertaining were somewhat different: the important thing was to cook a menu that you knew you could do, and which would impress; whereas nowadays I think a lot of us use friends as an excuse to experiment with something we wouldn't otherwise attempt!

EASY: *allow 45 minutes*

SERVES 6

25 g/1 oz butter, plus extra for greasing

1 onion, chopped

50 g/2 oz streaky bacon, chopped

2 tomatoes, chopped

50 g/2 oz mushrooms, chopped

75 ml/2½ fl oz milk

2 eggs, separated

175 g/6 oz Cheddar cheese, grated

salt and pepper

1 Preheat the oven to 190°C/170°C fan oven/Gas Mark 5. Butter six ramekin dishes, about 150 ml/¼ pint each.

2 Melt the butter and gently fry the onion until soft – about 5 minutes. Now add the bacon, tomatoes and mushrooms and cook for 5 minutes longer. Season well and put in the ramekins.

3 Place the milk, egg yolks and cheese in a pan and heat gently, stirring all the time, till the cheese has melted. You can leave it for an hour or so at room temperature at this stage, if convenient.

4 Whisk the egg whites till stiff and fold into the mixture. Pour into the ramekins.

5 Bake for 10–15 minutes till well risen and golden. Serve at once, with bread and butter.

HOME-MADE HUMUS

Humus, hummus, hoummous – spell it as you will, this delicious Middle-Eastern dip has captured the country. Everyone seems to buying a pack of crudités and dipping them in this subtle, creamy-beige substance.

HARDLY ANY COOKING: *allow 30 minutes; keeps for a week in the fridge*

SERVES 8

410 g can of chick-peas
2 large garlic cloves, peeled and
  roughly cut up
2 lemons
1 tbsp extra-virgin olive oil
1 tsp ground cumin
a pinch of cayenne pepper
150 ml/¼ pint tahini paste (sesame-
  seed paste, from delicatessens)
salt

To garnish:
extra-virgin olive oil
ground cumin
chopped fresh parsley
toasted pine kernels

❶ Simmer the chick-peas in their liquid for 10 minutes. Drain, reserving the liquid, and purée with the garlic, juice of the lemons, oil, cumin, cayenne and plenty of salt.

❷ Add the tahini paste and check the seasoning. Adjust to taste with more salt, lemon or oil, and adjust the consistency with extra tahini or some of the cooking water.

❸ Put into a bowl; dribble with a little extra oil, sprinkle with a little extra cumin and decorate with parsley and pine kernels.

T I P 🥣 One clever idea from the supermarkets: if you wish, you can stir a few whole chick-peas and pine kernels into the finished humus to add texture.

PEAR AND STILTON
TOASTED SANDWICH

Whenever I hear someone say 'do you know what my favourite secret treat is?' I prick up my ears. You can guarantee that you are going to be let in on some gem of a dish suitable for a quiet moment when you fancy a treat but don't want to go to any bother. Beans on toast with melted Red Leicester on top is one such delicacy, as is mushrooms fried, mixed with a little cream and paprika, also on toast.

This idea comes from Pat Steggall of Marlborough, Wiltshire – who says this is her absolute favourite lunch, and I agree it is delicious. Pat makes this with either a ripe or a canned pear. Even pears sold as 'ripe for eating' can still be a bit on the firm side, so I think a pear canned in natural juice is probably your best bet.

EASY: *grub's up in 20 minutes*

SERVES 1: EASILY DOUBLED

**2 slices of good white or brown
  bread – nothing too rustic
butter, for spreading
1 small, ripe pear, peeled and
  sliced, or 1 canned pear, sliced**

**25 g/1 oz Stilton cheese
a few sprigs of watercress,
  if you wish**

❶ Toast the bread under the grill on one side; then butter the toasted side.
❷ Arrange the pear and cheese (plus watercress, if using) on the toasted side of one slice, top with the other, toasted-side down, then grill each side until lightly browned – about 3–5 minutes per side. Serve hot.

STILTON-STUFFED MUSHROOMS

Everyone seems to love stuffed mushrooms, and this recipe is so good and tasty I serve it again and again. It makes a fine side dish for a barbecue, or an excellent first course for a supper party (you can put it in the oven and forget about it).

EASY: *allow 50 minutes, including 35 minutes baking*

SERVES 6–8 AS A FIRST COURSE

125 g/4 oz butter	1 tbsp chopped fresh sage
5 spring onions, chopped finely	2 tbsp chopped fresh parsley
150 g/5 oz white bread	6–8 large open-cap mushrooms
125 g/4 oz blue Stilton cheese,	(about 350 g/11 oz)
crumbled	

❶ Preheat the oven to 170°C/150°C fan oven/Gas Mark 3. Melt the butter in a saucepan, add the spring onions and soften for 3 minutes over a medium heat.

❷ Put the bread in a food processor and reduce to crumbs. Add the spring onions, cheese and herbs and process briefly till just combined (don't overdo this).

❸ Remove stems from the mushrooms (save for stock or discard – they are not wanted for this recipe). Press the stuffing lightly into the caps. Put on a greased baking tray and bake for 35 minutes.

T I P ☁ This is an unashamedly rich dish. If you wished, you could halve the butter and Stilton and fill the mushrooms more skimpily but, after eating it once, you will want the recipe in its original version every time!

TWICE-BAKED POTATOES

For every baked potato fan out there, here is the ultimate recipe for a tasty all-in-one supper. For flavour and satisfaction I don't think you can beat a good old-fashioned spud and, though this is a little more trouble than just splitting and sprinkling with cheese, it really does turn them into a gourmet feast.

EASY: *5 minutes to make, 1¹/₂ hours in the oven*

SERVES 4

4 × 275 g/9 oz baking potatoes, scrubbed, dried and rubbed lightly with oil

125 g/4 oz strong Cheddar cheese

200 ml/7 fl oz crème fraîche

2 tbsp butter, at room temperature

3 spring onions, chopped finely

¹/₂ tsp salt

freshly ground black pepper

1 Preheat the oven to 200°C/180°C fan oven/Gas Mark 6. Line a baking sheet with foil and bake the potatoes for 1 hour, till a skewer easily pierces the flesh. Set aside until cool enough to handle – about 10 minutes.

2 Wearing an oven glove, slice each potato in half to make two shallow halves. Scoop out most of flesh into a bowl, leaving 5 mm/¹/₄-inch thickness of flesh in each shell. Return the shells to the baking sheet and bake for 10 minutes.

3 Meanwhile, mash the potato flesh until smooth. Stir in the remaining ingredients, including seasoning.

4 Heat the grill. Pile the potato mixture into the shells and grill for 10–15 minutes. Allow to cool for 10 minutes before serving.

WILD MUSHROOM BRUSCHETTA

This recipe was gleaned from a smashing recipe book produced by the Friends of Guy's and Friends of St Thomas' Hospitals and there are many more recipes I shall be trying from it. If you want to buy your own copy, in an excellent cause, you can order one by sending a cheque for £8.95 plus £1.75 p&p to The Friends of St Thomas' Hospital, Lambeth Palace Road, London SE1 7EH. This recipe was contributed by the Head Chef of the hospitals' catering department, Hector.

If you haven't come across the term, bruschetta is Italian for a toasted snack.

EASY: *allow 10 minutes to prepare, 10 minutes to cook*

SERVES 4, AS AN APPETISER OR SNACK

50 g/2 oz butter

1 garlic clove, chopped

1 onion, chopped

500 g/1 lb wild mushrooms, sliced

a pinch of dried thyme

1 tsp chopped fresh parsley

4 slices of fresh bread, about
2 cm/¾ inch thick

1 whole garlic clove, halved

3 tbsp olive oil

salt and pepper

1 Put the butter in a frying pan, heat and add the chopped garlic – sizzle for half a minute and then add the onion and mushrooms. Cook vigorously for 5–10 minutes, till soft and beginning to brown. Stir in the thyme and parsley and season.

2 Meanwhile, toast the bread and rub quickly with the halved garlic clove.

3 Spread the mushroom mixture on the toast, sprinkle with pepper and drizzle with olive oil. If you wish, the toast can be cut in smaller pieces to serve with drinks.

ASPARAGUS AND PANCETTA SAUTÉ

Asparagus isn't with us for long, so enjoy it when you see it. As in many things, I am a bit of a traditionalist, and what I like best is very fresh, young British asparagus in the spring – not the imported sort that masquerades as British.

EASY: *45 minutes*

SERVES 4 – 6

1 tbsp olive oil

40 g/1½ oz pancetta, cut in small strips

2 small garlic cloves, sliced very thinly

25 g/1 oz butter

875 g/1¾ lb medium British asparagus (about 2–3 dozen spears), fibrous ends snapped off, stems peeled, rinsed and drained

lemon wedges, to serve

❶ Put a large frying pan over a medium heat and, when hot, add the olive oil and pancetta. Cook until light brown and slightly crisp (don't overdo this) – about 5 minutes. Remove from the heat and lift the pancetta with a slotted spoon on to kitchen paper to drain, leaving the fat in the pan.

❷ Put the pan back on the heat and cook the garlic for just 30 seconds, till fragrant but not golden. Use your slotted spoon to add to the pancetta.

❸ If you have less than 1 tbsp of fat in the pan at this point, make up with extra oil. Melt the butter in the pan and, when hot, add the asparagus. Season and sauté, stirring constantly, until the spears are light gold and tender (they will not brown evenly) but still slightly crisp. Watch and keep testing, but this will take 20–30 minutes.

❹ When cooked, return the pancetta and garlic to the pan to heat through with the asparagus. Serve with lemon wedges.

chapter 2

QUICK LUNCHES AND SUPPERS

My idea of a quick and easy supper depends on what time I've available, what I've got in the fridge and what I feel like doing, so this chapter includes a wide selection of suggestions to meet your different needs. Sometimes you've an hour spare in the morning, sometimes it's all got to be thrown together at the last minute. What all these dishes have in common is that they are comforting and delectable, and will quite certainly put smiles on any family's faces.

APRÈS-SKI SUPPER

This wonderful, rather rich supper is known in the French Alps as
tartiflette *and, since discovering it, I have tried it with different*
ingredients – each time with success. It's one of those dishes that is
great fun to make as well as eat, with no irksome lemons to zest and
hardly any chopping.

FUN TO MAKE: *ready in 45 minutes*

SERVES 4

375 g/12 oz potatoes, scrubbed
  but not peeled
25 g/1 oz butter
1 small onion, chopped
250 g/8 oz bacon, chopped

1 miniature Reblochon cheese, or
  half a big one (about 250–350 g)
5 tbsp single cream or milk
salt and pepper

❶ Preheat the oven to 220°C/200°C fan oven/Gas Mark 7. Boil the potatoes
in their skins in salted water for 15–20 minutes till tender; then peel if
you wish and thickly slice.

❷ While the potato is cooking, heat the butter in a frying pan and fry the
onion and bacon till lightly browned – about 5 minutes. Remove from the
pan and set aside. Add a little more butter, if necessary, and then add the
potato slices and brown for 2 minutes each side or till golden.

❸ Cut the cheese in half through the middle, then cube it, leaving the
crust on. Make layers of the potato, bacon and cheese in a buttered
gratin dish. Season as you go – go easy with the salt. Pour over the milk
or cream and bake for 20 minutes, till the top is brown and slightly
crisp. If necessary, brown under the grill briefly after baking. Serve with
a crisp green salad.

T I P 🥄 Reblochon is a particularly rich and smelly French
cheese that comes in a small wheel shape. It is worth seeking out
from a special cheese shop.

CHEDDAR AND SAUSAGE BAKE

This is one of those brilliant all-in-one supper dishes that is packed with flavour but a cinch to throw together. You can vary it in many ways and it may well become a family favourite.

EASY: *can be made ahead; 15 minutes to make, 2 hours to stand, 45 minutes in the oven*

SERVES 4

6 thick slices of french bread or
   other open-textured bread

3 large eggs

1 tsp Dijon mustard

½ tsp dried mixed herbs

½ tsp salt

284 ml carton of single cream

175 g/6 oz strong Cheddar cheese,
   grated

½ green pepper, cut in narrow
   strips

12 cherry tomatoes, halved

125 g/4 oz frankfurter or other
   cooked sausage, cut in chunks

2 tbsp chopped onion

freshly ground black pepper

chopped fresh parsley, to garnish

❶ Butter a 1.2-litre/2-pint baking dish – glass or china. Fit the bread on the bottom, cutting up as necessary to form a good base.

❷ Whisk the eggs, mustard, herbs and salt in a big bowl, then add the cream. Pour over the bread and leave at least 2 hours, or overnight.

❸ Preheat the oven to 180°C/160°C fan oven/Gas Mark 4. Grind a little black pepper over the egg mix, plus the half the cheese, the pepper, the tomatoes, sausage and onion, then finally the remaining cheese. Cover loosely with foil and bake for 30 minutes.

❹ Remove the foil and bake for another 20 minutes or so, till set and springy to the touch. Allow to cool for 5 minutes before serving, sprinkled with parsley.

TIP 🥣 For a vegetarian version, use olives instead of the sausage.

SIMPLE BROAD BEAN CASSOULET

In my early days as a passionate cook, one of my trademark dishes was an authentic French cassoulet and involved two days of fiddling and faffing. Life nowadays is run to a far stricter timetable and I can't think of any occasion when I would wish to spend two days on one dish. This recipe is an utterly delicious variation, using fresh broad beans instead of haricot beans.

STRAIGHTFORWARD: *allow 10 minutes to prepare, 1 hour to cook; freezes well*

SERVES 4 – 6

2 tbsp oil

6 herby sausages

500 g/1 lb lamb fillet, cut in
   2.5 cm/ 1-inch pieces

1 onion, chopped

2 garlic cloves, chopped finely

875 g/1¾ lb fresh, ripe tomatoes,
   chopped roughly (no need to skin)

275 g/9 oz broad beans – weighed
   after podding (about double that
   weight before podding)

a large knob of butter

75 g/3 oz white breadcrumbs

3 tbsp chopped fresh parsley

1 Heat the oil in a large frying pan and fry the sausages till browned – about 6–7 minutes. Remove from the pan and add the lamb: brown all over. (If your pan isn't large enough, brown the lamb in batches.)

2 Remove from the pan and add the onion. Cook for 6–7 minutes, till browned, adding garlic for last minute. Return the sausages and lamb, with the tomatoes. Bring to the boil and then simmer, uncovered, for 30–35 minutes, till the liquid has reduced and thickened. Add broad beans for last 10 minutes of cooking time.

3 Meanwhile, melt the butter and fry the breadcrumbs and parsley till golden – 3–4 minutes. Sprinkle over the meat-bean mixture and serve.

GOLDEN KEDGEREE

This dish was inspired by lunch at the Ivy, one of London's most perennially fashionable restaurants, where – to be quite honest – the clientele tends to attract more attention than the food. On the menu was kedgeree, which inspired me to reacquaint myself with this wonderful Anglo-Indian dish.

EASY, BUT A FAIR AMOUNT OF WASHING UP: *30 minutes to prepare, 20 minutes in the oven to finish*

SERVES 4

a good pinch of saffron strands

125 g/4 oz long-grain rice

225 g/8 oz smoked haddock or other smoked fish

a small knob of butter and 2 tsp olive oil

1 onion, sliced finely

½ tsp curry powder or 1 tsp curry paste

2 eggs, hard-boiled and shelled

To garnish:

paprika, for sprinkling

chopped fresh parsley (optional)

❶ Bring salted water to the boil, add the saffron and boil the rice for 15 minutes. Test and drain if done.

❷ Meanwhile, depending on its thickness, poach the fish for 5–10 minutes in enough water to cover, until tender. Drain, remove skin and flake the flesh.

❸ Fry the onion in the oil and butter for 7 minutes, till tender, sprinkling with the curry powder or paste halfway through.

❹ Fold the rice, fish and onion together and put in serving dish. Quarter the shelled eggs and, using a spoon, push them into the kedgeree at intervals (otherwise they break up). Warm through in the oven for 20 minutes and serve sprinkled with paprika and fresh parsley, if you wish.

PUMPKIN AND CHICKEN GRATIN

I am very fond of gratins – grilled dishes with a crunchy topping. Any French title is inclined to sound fancy – which gratins most certainly aren't – but the alternative is 'bake', which sounds rather plodding.

EASY: *allow 30 minutes to prepare, 45 minutes to cook*

SERVES 4

1 kg/2 lb pumpkin (weighed before preparing)	2 tbsp mild curry paste
	2 egg yolks
200 ml/7 fl oz cream	1 tbsp curry powder
2 courgettes	1 tbsp dried breadcrumbs
2 tomatoes	50 g/2 oz butter
4 boneless chicken breasts, skinned or skinless as you wish	salt and pepper
	1 tbsp paprika, to garnish
3 tbsp oil	

❶ Peel the pumpkin with a sharp knife, remove seeds and stringy bits and cube the flesh. Cook in the cream for about 20 minutes, until reduced to a thickish sauce – do not liquidise. Season well and set aside.

❷ Preheat the oven to 180°C/160°C fan oven/Gas Mark 4. Cut the courgettes and tomatoes into large dice. Cut the chicken breasts into strips. Heat the oil in a pan and fry the chicken, courgettes, tomatoes and curry paste gently for 15 minutes, stirring from time to time, then put this into a buttered gratin dish. Cover with the pumpkin purée.

❸ Mix the egg yolks, curry powder and breadcrumbs and spread over the pumpkin. Dot with butter and bake for 25 minutes. Remove from oven and dust with paprika to serve.

> **TIP** 🥣 Pumpkins are not always easy to find so you can buy a different sort of squash (such as butternut squash) if convenient. Or buy a small pumpkin when you next spot one and keep in a cool place till the time comes to cook it – they keep for at least two to three weeks.

GREEN AND WHITE FETTUCINE

This is a rich but very straightforward pasta recipe for when you want something de luxe but feel like a break from fancy flavours and complicated cooking.

CAN'T GO WRONG: *allow 30 minutes – serve at once*

SERVES 4

125 g/4 oz dried plain fettucine or other pasta

125 g/4 oz dried green fettucine or other pasta (see Tip)

125 g/4 oz butter

1 garlic clove, chopped

250 ml/8 fl oz whipping cream

2 tbsp chopped fresh parsley

300 g/10 oz frozen peas, thawed

50 g/2 oz freshly grated parmesan cheese, plus extra for sprinkling

250 g/8 oz cooked ham, cut in fine strips

freshly ground black pepper

❶ Cook both lots of pasta together in a large pan of boiling water till just tender. Drain and set aside.

❷ Meanwhile, melt the butter in a pan until sizzling and add the garlic, stirring. After just 2–3 minutes (no longer – you want the garlic to be just pale golden, not at all brown), stir in the cream, parsley, peas and black pepper. Bring to a simmer for 3–5 minutes.

❸ Stir in the cooked pasta, cheese and ham. Heat through until the cheese has melted and you can resist no longer. Serve with extra cheese sprinkled over.

T I P ⬯ It is safest to buy white and green pasta from the same brand, with the same recommended cooking time, for this recipe, as you want to be sure they will both be cooked simultaneously. Mind you, I do not always believe the timings on the packets – sometimes they're too long, sometimes too short – so I always test carefully with a type that is new to me.

HERBY MEAT LOAF

In the autumn and winter I feel the need for tasty comfort food that more or less cooks itself. This recipe has quite a few ingredients but is dead easy to make; leftovers are a real plus as they reheat perfectly, or you can freeze them in portions and microwave them for quick suppers. EASY: *allow 30 minutes to make, 1¹/4 hours in the oven*

SERVES 6, GENEROUSLY

15 g/¹/₂ oz dried mushrooms

250 ml/8 fl oz boiling water

2 tbsp butter

1 onion, chopped finely

3 large garlic cloves, crushed

2 tbsp finely chopped fresh
rosemary (see Tip)

2 tsp finely chopped fresh thyme

1 tsp finely chopped fresh sage

4 slices of white bread, crusts
removed

500 g/1 lb minced beef

500 g/1 lb minced pork

50 g/2 oz ham, chopped finely

2 large eggs, beaten lightly

1 tbsp salt

1 tsp freshly ground black pepper

1 tbsp mayonnaise

1¹/₂ tsp Dijon mustard

a pinch of cayenne pepper

For the mushroom gravy (optional):

175 g/6 oz mushrooms, sliced thinly

1 small onion, or 2 spring onions,
chopped

1 tbsp plain flour, mixed with
2 tbsp water

175 ml/6 fl oz chicken stock

75 ml/2¹/₂ fl oz white wine

salt and pepper

❶ Soak the dried mushrooms in the water for about 20 minutes. Lift out the mushrooms with a slotted spoon and pour the soaking liquid into a small bowl, leaving grit behind.

❷ Preheat the oven to 180°C/160°C fan oven/Gas Mark 4. Melt half the butter in a medium frying pan and cook the onion for 5 minutes, then add the garlic, chopped dried mushrooms and 2 tbsp of the soaking liquid; cook for 5 minutes. Stir in the herbs and scrape into a bowl.

❸ Soak the bread in the remaining liquid then squeeze dry and tear up roughly, saving the liquid for the gravy. Add the bread to the cooked onions, along with the meat and eggs. Season with the salt and pepper. Knead and put into a 25×15 cm/10×6-inch baking tin (see Tips). Mix the mayo with the mustard and cayenne and brush over the top. Then bake for 1¼ hours or until browned and firm. When cooked, turn out and use the tin to make the gravy.

❹ Melt the butter in the roasting tin and fry the mushrooms and onion for 5 minutes, then stir in the flour. Add the stock, wine and remaining soaking liquid gradually, whisking all the time. Season and serve with thick slices of the meat loaf.

T I P S 🥣 If you don't have fresh herbs at your fingertips, use 2 tsp dried mixed herbs.

If you don't have the right size roasting tin, use any baking dish.

The gravy can be made in a pan, but it is extra delicious with the caramelised bits of meat loaf in it.

GREEN BEAN AND HAM GRATIN

I dedicate this dish to every keen gardener who ends up with a mountain of beans and a shortage of ideas for what to do with them! The nice thing about this dish is that the beans make a major contribution, rather than just being an accompaniment.

EASY: *allow 10 minutes to prepare, 30 minutes to cook*

SERVES 4

500 g/1 lb green beans	400 g can of cannellini beans,
25 g/1 oz butter	drained and rinsed
a bunch of spring onions, cut in	200 ml tub of crème fraîche (see Tip)
2 cm/¾-inch pieces	3 tbsp chopped fresh parsley
175 g/6 oz thick slice of ham,	3 tbsp snipped fresh chives
cut in chunks	4 tbsp freshly grated parmesan cheese

1 Preheat the oven to 200°C/180°C fan oven/Gas Mark 6. Trim the green beans, then plunge them into a large pan of boiling, salted water. Cook for 2 minutes until tender-crisp. Drain then refresh under cold running water.

2 Melt the butter in a large pan, add the spring onions, ham and cannellini beans and allow to heat through. Stir in the green beans, then transfer to a medium shallow gratin dish.

3 Mix together the crème fraîche and the herbs. Season well with salt and pepper, then spread the herby crème fraîche over the top of the beans and sprinkle with the cheese. Bake for 25–30 minutes, until the cheese has melted and is golden. Serve with bread to mop up the juices.

TIP Make sure you use full-fat crème fraîche, as this will melt to make a smooth creamy sauce. Half-fat crème fraîche doesn't give a good result for most cooking purposes.

HACHIS FLAMAND

This is a shepherd's pie with a difference. Hachis *is French for mince, and* flamand *denotes this idea comes from Flanders. In any case it is a delicious tasty supper dish for four, topped not with the customary potatoes but a cream and cheese mixture.*

Gruyère is an expensive cheese and I find that Cheddar makes an excellent substitute. But for the full authentic (and admittedly very pungent) effect, do try Gruyère if you can get it. It will transport you instantly across the Channel.

EASY: *ready in an hour, including 20 minutes baking*

SERVES 4

50 g/2 oz butter	2 tbsp oil
5 leeks, cleaned and sliced	4 tbsp Dijon mustard – less if
2 slices of bacon, cut up small	using English
2 onions, chopped	142 ml carton of cream
500 g/1 lb minced beef	250 g/8 oz Gruyère cheese, grated

❶ Preheat the oven to 220°C/200°C fan oven/Gas Mark 7. In a large saucepan or large deep frying pan, melt the butter and cook the leeks until soft; add the bacon and cook for 15 minutes.

❷ Heat the oil in another pan and sauté the onions until soft; add the meat, salt and pepper and cook for 10 minutes gently. Add the mustard and half the cream and put in a gratin dish. Now cover with the leek-and-bacon mixture.

❸ Mix the remaining cream with the cheese and spread over the mixture. Bake for 20 minutes, till melted, and serve hot.

> **TIP** 🥣 Mince has something of a bad name and, indeed, the worst sort is cheap and fatty. Buy the best you can find.

HADDOCK AND CABBAGE LASAGNE

A slightly unusual ingredient combination makes for a succulent, low-fat winter supper.

STRAIGHTFORWARD: *allow 30 minutes to make, 50 minutes to cook; freezes well*

SERVES 6

250 g/8 oz instant or fresh lasagne (see Tip)	875 g/1¾ lb fresh haddock fillets
	500 ml/18 fl oz milk
1 green cabbage, washed, cored and leaves separated	125 g/4 oz Edam or other low-fat cheese, sliced thinly
25 g/1 oz butter	salt and pepper

❶ Cook the cabbage leaves for 5 minutes in boiling, salted water. Then squeeze dry, chop finely and fry in the butter for 20–25 minutes.

❷ Meanwhile, cut the haddock into cubes and put in a saucepan. Cover with the milk and poach for about 7–8 minutes. Remove haddock from pan (reserving milk) and discard skin. Preheat the oven to 180°C/160°C fan oven/Gas Mark 4.

❸ Take a 20 × 25 cm/8 × 10-inch shallow dish. Put a layer of cabbage in the bottom, then fish, then lasagne, seasoning as you go. Repeat, finishing with a layer of lasagne.

❹ Pour the reserved milk over the top and then cover with the cheese slices. Bake for 20 minutes, until hot and melted.

T I P 🥣 If you have a choice, use lasagne that does not need precooking and can be baked from raw. If the packet indicates you do need to preboil it, however, do this before you start the rest of the recipe and leave on racks to cool so the sheets don't stick together.

JERUSALEM ARTICHOKES WITH BACON AND CHEESE

This dish makes an interesting accompaniment or stylish supper in its own right. Jerusalem artichokes remain exotic and unusual even though (as you will know if you have a vegetable garden) they are furiously invasive, and ungetriddable once established.

EASY: *15 minutes*

SERVES 4

500 g/1 lb jerusalem artichokes   **125 g/4 oz hard goat's cheese,**
2 bacon rashers   **grated coarsely**
                                              salt and freshly ground black pepper

❶ Peel the artichokes, cut up roughtly and boil in salted water until completely tender – about 10–15 minutes.

❷ Meanwhile, slice the bacon into strips and fry for about 5 minutes, till brown. Add the drained, roughly mashed artichokes (do this with a fork in the colander) and stir well in the pan so all the brown bits are absorbed into the mixture.

❸ So far can be done in advance. At the last minute, stir in the coarsely grated cheese and freshly ground black pepper.

T I P S 🥄 Artichokes go brown if left for any period, but this is not a concern here as you cook them immediately. If you specially want them to stay creamy white, for instance in a soup, then drop them into water with a good dash of vinegar to stop them oxidising.

When I first started cooking, artichokes were amazingly nobbly and dreadful to peel. I don't know if they are growing different varieties, or if greengrocers pick out the nice oval ones specially for us, but the shapes nowadays are no trouble at all and they are no harder to peel than potatoes.

LEMON CHICKEN

This recipe has a point of technical interest that will appeal to those cooks who like to do the thing properly and brown meat, chicken or fish before cooking it through fully. This procedure is the classic way to start most stews and casseroles, the idea being that the meat is 'sealed' and the juices kept in.

Technically that isn't quite what happens: what actually occurs is that the flavours of the meat are dramatically enhanced by being subjected to the quick burst of heat when they are fried, and browning is the outward sign of that flavour enhancement.

Interestingly, if using a non-stick pan, up to the minute advice is that browning is best achieved by laying the food in the hot oil and not touching it or moving it in any way till browning has been achieved. This will amaze those cooks who like to shift the food around in the pan solicitously to stop it sticking – but try it and see. The food will not stick, the browning will be richer and quicker and the food taste better at the end of the cooking.

WORTH THE TROUBLE: *allow 30 minutes; freezes well*

•

SERVES 4, GENEROUSLY

2 large lemons, preferably unwaxed

4 boneless, skinless chicken breasts, preferably free-range, sliced in thin strips

4 tbsp plain flour

4 tbsp vegetable oil

1 small shallot, chopped finely, or a small garlic clove, chopped finely, as you prefer

250 ml/8 fl oz chicken stock

2 tbsp small capers, drained (optional)

3 tbsp butter

2 tbsp finely chopped fresh parsley

salt and pepper

❶ Warm the oven gently and put a large heatproof plate on the rack. Halve a lemon. Trim end from one half and cut in very thin slices – set aside. Juice the remaining half and the whole lemon.

❷ Season the chicken. Put the flour into a plastic bag and, adding one piece of chicken at a time, shake to coat. Lay the flour-coated chicken on a board.

❸ Heat a frying pan till hot and add 2 tbsp of the oil. Put half the chicken pieces in the pan and fry without shifting them for 2½ minutes, then turn over for the same on the other side. Check they are cooked. Remove to the hot plate in the oven, then repeat with remaining oil and chicken pieces.

❹ Add the shallot or garlic to the pan and fry for half a minute. Add the stock and lemon slices, and simmer till reduced to about 2–3 tbsp (about 4 minutes). Add the lemon juice and capers, if using, and simmer till again reduced, then swirl in the butter and whisk (the sauce will thicken slightly at this point). Stir in the parsley.

❺ Spoon the sauce over the chicken and serve at once, accompanied by rice or the trendy new rice/pasta alternative called Ebly or 'pasta wheat' (which is rather like pearl barley but cooks in 15 minutes).

T I P I am aware that many people have a great dislike of capers (anchovies are similarly controversial). I like them, though not in everything, but this dish works without them.

MEDITERRANEAN
MEATBALLS

Meatballs are a delicious way to jazz up good old mince; here they are livened up by the addition of pine kernels, which add a crunch.

EASY: *allow 30 minutes to prepare, 25 minutes to cook; freezes well*

SERVES 4 – 6

25 g/1 oz pine kernels

2 bacon rashers

1 onion

1 small red pepper (optional)

1 garlic clove

500 g/1 lb raw minced beef or lamb

50 g/2 oz fresh white breadcrumbs
 (about 2 medium slices)

a good pinch of dried mixed herbs

salt, pepper, Tabasco sauce,
 Worcestershire sauce and
 ketchup, as you wish

1 medium egg

2 tbsp olive oil, for frying

200 ml/7 fl oz bought or home-made
 tomato sauce, to serve

❶ Toast the pine kernels in a large frying pan for about 5 minutes till light brown, tossing frequently (no oil necessary). Remove to a small bowl.

❷ Finely chop the bacon, onion, pepper and garlic and fry for about 8 minutes till brown (again, no need to add oil).

❸ Mix the pine kernels, fried mixture, meat, crumbs, herbs, plentiful seasoning and egg – it's easiest to use your hands. Form into about 20 small balls the size of walnuts. Don't get impatient and make them too large, as you will merely waste extra time cooking them. You can do all this in advance, or cook at once.

❹ Preheat the oven to 180°C/160°C fan oven/Gas Mark 4. Heat the oil and fry the balls in two batches for about 5 minutes per batch; transfer to an ovenproof dish when cooked and finish cooking in the oven for about 15 minutes. Heat the tomato sauce to a simmer and pour over. Serve with baked potatoes or as they do in the United States, spaghetti.

MUSTARD MASH WITH SAUSAGES

This recipe is a really substantial accompaniment to pork chops, roast pork or other meat dishes; if you have a family, and perhaps the constant battle to keep teenagers fed, then this is the answer. It is also excellent food for a gathering, as there is nothing tricky about it and people just can't resist it.

EASY: *ready in an hour but not too much work*

SERVES 4 (EASILY DOUBLED)

1 kg/2 lb King Edward or Maris Piper potatoes, peeled and cut in chunks

125 g/4 oz British 'country-style' sausages (coarse-textured), slipped out of their skins and crumbled

150 ml/¼ pint milk

2 tbsp wholegrain mustard

3 tbsp butter, at room temperature

1 Cook the potatoes, in plenty of salted water, until tender – about 20 minutes. Drain well and return to pan.

2 Meanwhile, cook the sausage meat in a frying pan without added fat until browned through – 8 minutes. Add the milk and mustard to this pan and bring to a simmer.

3 Mash the potatoes. Gradually mix in the milk/sausage mixture, then add the butter and stir to melt. Season and serve.

T I P Sausages are easier to get out of their skins, and easier to handle generally, if well chilled.

PASTA ALL'AMATRICIANA

This is one of the greatest storecupboard pasta suppers and, although it has a complicated name (it is the local dish of Amatrice, near Rome), is really very simple.

EASY: *on the table in 40 minutes*

SERVES 4

3 tbsp extra-virgin olive oil

175 g/6 oz rinded streaky smoked bacon (see Tips)

1 medium onion, chopped finely

½ tsp dried chilli flakes (see Tips)

1½ × 400 g can of tomatoes in natural juices (in other words, 600 g)

500 g/1 lb dried linguine or other long, fine pasta

40 g/1½ oz parmesan cheese, grated

salt and pepper

❶ Bring a large pot of salted water to the boil for the pasta.

❷ Meanwhile, heat the oil in a large frying pan and, when hot, cook the bacon till brown and crisp – about 8 minutes. Transfer with a slotted spoon to a plate lined with paper towels. In the remaining oil, soften the onion – about 5 minutes. Add the chilli and cook for 30 seconds, then the tomatoes and salt to taste. Simmer for 10 minutes, till thickened.

❸ Cook the pasta, drain and return to the pot.

❹ Nearly ready to serve: add the bacon to the tomato sauce, adjust the seasoning and toss with the pasta. Add the cheese, toss again and serve.

T I P 🥣 If you have an Italian delicatessen in your area, use finely sliced pancetta instead of the bacon. You do not need to cut the rind off pancetta – it seems to disappear as you cook it. You can buy it in little cubes or lardons in the supermarket but, to be honest, I find these rather tough and gristly.

PASTA WITH CREAMY TOMATO AND SAUSAGE SAUCE

My recipe timings are based on actual time spent preparing, cooking and mixing. They do not include shopping, getting out ingredients, washing up – nor indeed phonecalls while you are cooking, stopping for a cuppa and so on. My tester and I are not supercooks and we have normal domestic kitchens. If I really rush I can usually shave about 10–20 per cent off a recipe timing, but that is not what our timings are based on. After all, cooking should be enjoyable, not a battle.

STRAIGHTFORWARD: *allow 40 minutes, including cooking*

SERVES 4

2 tbsp olive oil	1 tbsp dried sage
1 onion, chopped	½ tsp dried crushed chillies or
2 large garlic cloves, chopped	chilli powder
500 g/1 lb sausages, out of their skins	375 g/12 oz dried fettuccine or
250 ml/8 fl oz whipping cream	tagliatelle
2 × 400 g cans of tomatoes in	50 g/2 oz parmesan cheese, grated,
natural juice	to serve

❶ Heat the oil in a large saucepan over medium heat. Add the onion and garlic and sauté for 3 minutes. Add the sausages and cook for 5 minutes or till no longer pink, breaking up the meat with the back of a fork. Add the cream and simmer for 5 minutes; then add the tomatoes, sage and chilli. Simmer until it thickens slightly – about 15 minutes.

❷ Meanwhile, cook the pasta in a large pot of boiling, salted water according to packet instructions. Drain, reserving a little of the cooking water. Return the pasta to the pot and stir in the sauce. Toss together, adding a little of the cooking water if the pasta looks at all dry. Sprinkle with cheese and serve.

PORTUGUESE LAMB

This recipe is by Sheila Pennant Jones, who is a volunteer at Guy's Hospital, and I was introduced to it when I launched their charity cookbook at the hospital (see page 22).

EASY: *takes 15–20 minutes*

SERVES 2

2 lamb chump chops

50 g/2 oz butter

1 tsp wholegrain mustard

1 tsp Worcestershire Sauce

1 tbsp dry sherry

1½ tbsp double cream

salt and pepper

❶ Season the chops well and fry in the butter for 15–20 minutes, till cooked. Meanwhile, mix the mustard, Worcestershire Sauce and sherry.

❷ Remove the chops from the pan and keep them warm. Pour away fat from the pan but leave any tasty crusty bits. Stir in the sauce mixture and whisk like mad.

❸ When hot, stir in the cream, check the seasoning, bring just to the boil and serve poured over the chops.

TIP 🥣 You can use the same sauce for chicken or pork chops, but make sure the meat is fully cooked before removing in step 2.

POTATO AND BACON HASH

This easy supper dish fits the bill when you are looking for something comforting but not at all rich; if you are serving four, make two hashes rather than trying to jam it all in one saucepan.

You will notice the recipe calls for new potatoes but if you only have old potatoes in your vegetable rack then they will do as well. Slice them thickly for the boiling, try not to overboil them and make sure you use a non-stick pan when frying as floury potatoes have a tendency to stick.

CAN'T GO WRONG: *allow 30 minutes*

SERVES 2

500 g/1 lb new potatoes

50 g/2 oz bacon, smoked or
  unsmoked (see Tip), cut in strips

25 g/1 oz butter

1 small onion, chopped finely
chopped fresh parsley

❶ Boil the potatoes in salted water till just tender; then cool and slice fairly thickly.

❷ In a medium frying pan, preferably non-stick, dry-fry the bacon for 2 minutes, or till crisp – about 7 minutes. Transfer to a plate.

❸ Melt the butter in the pan, add the potatoes and fry, turning occasionally, until golden and crisp, 7 minutes again. Add the onion and bacon, season and cook for a further 5 minutes, till the onion looks translucent.

❹ Stir in the parsley and pile on to plates. A fried egg makes a luxurious finishing touch but is by no means necessary.

> **T I P** 🥣 This recipe is even better with pancetta, smoked Italian bacon with a particularly pungent flavour. Ask the delicatessen to slice it very thinly for you – they will usually interleave it with thin plastic film. I often buy a batch and pop it in the freezer in the bag it comes in.

SALAMI AND GORGONZOLA PIZZA

There is no comparison between a bought frozen pizza, complete with skimpy topping, and one made with love and care. If you wish you can even make the base but pizza mixes are easy and popular. Alternatively, you can buy a part-cooked base for this recipe.

EASY: *allow 40 minutes*

MAKES TWO 23cm/9-inch, GENEROUS PIZZAS

2 × 23 cm/9-inch half-baked pizza crusts

300 ml jar tomato sauce – your choice of flavour

175 g/6 oz mozzarella cheese, grated (see Tip)

a handful of fresh basil leaves, sliced thinly

375 g/12 oz salami sausage, sliced and rind cut off

125 g/4 oz Gorgonzola cheese, crumbled

2 tbsp black olives, pitted and halved

4 thin rounds of green pepper (or use marinated peppers from a jar of antipasto)

❶ Preheat the oven to 220°C/200°C fan oven/Gas Mark 7.

❷ Put the pizza crusts on rimless baking sheets. Leaving a 2 cm/¾-inch border, spread one-third of the sauce over the base of the first crust and another third over the base of the second. Sprinkle the mozzarella, three-quarters of the basil and the salami and Gorgonzola over the two pizzas, then top with the olives and peppers. Drizzle with the remaining sauce.

❸ Bake until the crust is crisp and golden and the topping hot and melting – about 15 minutes. Serve sprinkled with the remaining basil.

TIP 🥣 Mozzarella comes in many shapes and forms. For eating on its own as a salad, the buffalo version (it really is made with from buffalo milk) is incomparable – mild and tender. For cooked versions, or grating, use the block version you find wrapped in plastic.

SEAFOOD PAELLA

Here is a low-fat treat adapted from Sue Ashworth's excellent Pure
Points Cookbook *for Weight Watchers (Simon and Schuster, £10.99;
call the Express Bookshop on 0870 366 6092). Over the years I have
tried to slim down my recipes and, though there is something to be
said for the philosophy of merely eating less rather than adapting the
way you cook; in some recipes you simply don't notice the lack of fat.*
EASY: *allow 40 minutes*

SERVES 4

1 tsp olive oil

1 small onion, chopped finely

1 garlic clove, crushed

a pinch of saffron strands

1 red pepper, de-seeded and sliced

250 g/8 oz risotto rice

900 ml/1½ pints fish or vegetable
stock

150 g/5 oz frozen peas

250 g/8 oz skinless cod fillet,
cut in bite-size pieces

150 g/5 oz prawns

2 tbsp chopped fresh parsley

❶ Heat the oil in a large pan and add the onion and garlic. Cook until
softened but not browned – about 5 minutes.

❷ Put the saffron in a cup and pour over 2 tbsp boiling water. Leave
to infuse.

❸ Add the pepper and rice to the frying pan, with the saffron and its
water and the stock. Simmer for 15 minutes, until most of the liquid has
been absorbed. Rice does vary, so be prepared to add a little extra stock
or boiling water if the mixture starts to look dry.

❹ Add the peas and fish and cook on for 5 minutes. Toss in the prawns
and parsley, season and heat till piping hot.

> **TIP** 🥄 If cooking the peas and prawns from frozen, add a
> couple of minutes to the cooking time to make sure the paella is
> really good and hot.

SMOKED SALMON AND TOMATO PASTA

*Most of my recipes are born from careful thought and scrupulous testing.
The way it works is that I come up with the original idea and try it
out – often in a real situation, such as a lunch or weekend supper.
Once I am happy with it, I write it all out and send it off to my
official tester (none other than my mother). She makes the dish from
scratch, following my recipe to the letter, and reports back with myriad
changes, suggestions and corrections. If she can't find an ingredient
easily in her local shop or supermarket, she tells me. If there is
something tricky about a technique, she comes up with a solution.*

*This recipe is something of an exception, in that it was created one
evening when a friend dropped round unexpectedly. Not wishing to
go out, I promised to whizz something up in the kitchen – before
looking in the fridge, which contained precisely some smoked salmon I
had been given as a gift, half a pound of tomatoes, plain yogurt and
some Cheddar cheese. We had even run out of milk! Using my wits I
created this dish, and I was so pleased with it (specially the low-fat
sauce, made using plain yogurt), that I share it with you now. It goes
without saying that, like every recipe in this book, it was put through
the meticulous Patsy Murrin test procedure.*

EASY: *ready in 30 minutes*

SERVES 4

250 g/8 oz small, ripe tomatoes, sliced

1 tbsp oil

200 g/7 oz farfalle or other pasta
   shapes

1 tsp cornflour

142 ml carton of plain yogurt

50 g/2 oz Cheddar cheese, grated

125 g/4 oz smoked salmon
   trimmings, chopped

2 tbsp vodka or aquavit (optional)

Tabasco sauce

salt, pepper and sugar

1 Cook the tomatoes in the oil gently in a pan for 7–8 minutes till soft and wet. Season with salt, pepper and a little sugar.

2 Cook the pasta as directed.

3 Stir the cornflour into the yogurt and mix well. Add to the tomatoes and stir in; simmer gently for a minute or two.

4 Drain the pasta, keeping a cup of the cooking water in case you need it in the next step. Shake it dry but not too dry and stir in the tomato sauce to coat, followed by the cheese and smoked salmon. Heat through, stirring all the time, season well and then transfer to hot plates.

5 Sprinkle with vodka or aquavit, if you like, to add a Northern touch, and a good splash of Tabasco and serve. It does not need parmesan or further embellishment.

T I P If you don't have vodka or aquavit you can use gin – or omit altogether.

SPICY SAUSAGE AND PORK CASSEROLE

This recipe is a quick family supper that you can throw together in just over half an hour. At well under £1 per serving it is a bargain, and if you can find kabanos sausages – spicy Continental style – you will be introducing the family to an ingredient that is new and fashionable.
EASY: *allow 35 minutes*

SERVES 4

1 tbsp oil	2 kabanos sausages, sliced thickly,
4 pork shoulder steaks, cut in cubes	or any other spicy sausage
1 onion, chopped	400 g can of chopped tomatoes
2 garlic cloves, chopped	400 g can of butter beans, drained
	country bread, to serve

❶ Heat the oil in a large casserole or saucepan. Add the pork and cook, stirring, until browned all over. Remove from the pan and add the onion. Cook for 5 minutes until beginning to brown. Stir in the garlic and sausages. Tip in the tomatoes and bring to the boil.

❷ Reduce the heat and simmer for 10 minutes, until the pork is cooked through. Stir in the butter beans and heat through. Serve with plenty of country bread to soak up the juices.

TIP 🥄 'Country bread' or pain de campagne, is a generic term for rough, open-textured bread. Used to mop up the rich juices of the casserole, it should not need butter.

SWEETCORN AND BACON TART

If you use ready-made or ready-rolled pastry, don't omit the baking blind in step 1, which is critical to give the pastry its crunchy base.

WORTH THE TROUBLE: *allow 30 minutes to prepare, 25 minutes to cook*

SERVES 8

175 g/6 oz plain flour

75 g/3 oz butter

1 egg yolk

salt

For the filling:

75 g/3 oz bacon, rinded and
    snipped into small strips

3 ears of sweetcorn, kernels
    stripped off with a sharp knife
    (about 200 g/7 oz kernels) or

200g/7oz canned sweetcorn,
    drained

2 large eggs

150 g Boursin soft cheese with
    garlic and herbs

50 g/2 oz cheese, grated

142 ml carton of single cream

½ tsp crushed chillies (optional)

salt and pepper

❶ Preheat the oven to 190°C/170°C fan oven/Gas Mark 5. Make the pastry by rubbing the butter into the flour and adding seasoning and just enough water to bind – or do this in a food processor. Shape into a disc and chill for 30 minutes in the fridge or 10 minutes in the freezer if you're in a hurry.

❷ Roll out the pastry and line a 34 × 11 cm/13½ × 4-inch, loose-based, fluted tin, or a deep, 23 cm/9-inch round fluted tin. Bake blind, using baking parchment and beans, for 20 minutes. Lower oven heat to 180°C/160°C fan oven/Gas Mark 4.

❸ Meanwhile, dry-fry the bacon for 5 minutes, till beginning to go golden, and then add the corn. Cook for 3–4 minutes, till the corn is just tender. Beat the eggs, cheeses and cream with seasoning and the crushed chillies, if using. Add the corn and bacon and pour into the pastry case. Bake for 25 minutes, till just set: the filling should still be very tender, though not liquid. Leave to cool and serve warm.

TAGLIATELLE CARBONARA

*I have cooked spaghetti carbonara a dozen different ways, but this –
which I learnt from Italian chef Aldo Zilli – is the best.*

EASY: *allow 25 minutes*

SERVES 4

75 g/3 oz butter

125 g/4 oz pancetta or unsmoked
  bacon, cut in strips

400 g/14 oz dried tagliatelle

8 egg yolks

6 tbsp double cream

50 g/2 oz parmesan cheese,
  freshly grated

1 tsp freshly ground black pepper

½ tsp freshly grated nutmeg

2 tbsp chopped fresh parsley

❶ Bring a large pan of salted water to the boil. Melt the butter in a large,
deep frying pan and cook the pancetta or bacon till golden – 3 minutes
or so.

❷ Add the pasta to the boiling water and boil till *al dente* – about 8
minutes but check the packet as brands vary. Meanwhile, in a large
bowl, beat all the remaining ingredients till mixed.

❸ Drain the pasta. Remove the pancetta from the heat and add the
pasta to it, mixing quickly with the pancetta and the butter it's been
frying in.

❹ Tip the pasta mixture into the bowl containing the egg mixture and
toss well. The heat from the pasta and bacon will gently cook the eggs.
Serve immediately.

T I P The egg whites from this dish can be kept for meringues,
added to omelettes and so on to lighten up the mixture, or frozen.
If you freeze them, I find it makes sense to mark on the freezer bag
how many egg whites are there, and what size the eggs were.

ARTICHOKE AND SPINACH GRATIN

This is a wonderful, easy, vegetarian main course – ideal for summer entertaining. The original version, which comes from Provence in the south of France – includes fresh artichokes, which require complicated preparation, but I have used the excellent ones in jars, or canned ones as you wish.

EASY: *allow 1 hour*

SERVES 6

2 × 300 g/10 oz bags of fresh spinach
2 garlic cloves, chopped
2 × 280 g jars of artichoke hearts or
 2 × 400 g cans, drained and rinsed

150 g/5 oz Gruyère or Cheddar
 cheese, grated

❶ Preheat the oven to 190°C/170°C fan oven/Gas Mark 5. Heat a large, non-stick pan over a medium heat. Add the spinach in batches, turning frequently, until wilted. Drain well. Combine the spinach and garlic.

❷ Put the artichokes in a 28 × 18 cm/11 × 7-inch baking dish, brushed with oil to prevent sticking. Add a layer of spinach on top of the artichokes. Sprinkle with 50 g/2 oz of the cheese. Repeat layers of artichoke and spinach. Cover loosely with foil and bake for 15 minutes, then for 30 minutes with foil removed. Now sprinkle with the remaining cheese and bake for a final 10 minutes, till golden.

TIP This dish is technically a *tian* – a French term for a gratin (usually vegetable) and also the earthenware dish it is cooked in. This linguistic foible is by no means rare in French – a *casserole* is the name of the recipe and of the pot it is cooked in, and the same goes for *terrine* and indeed gratin.

CREAMY CHICKEN AND MUSHROOMS

Although this half-hour supper is creamy in texture, it is not a rich and fattening dish, and you can trim the calories even further by using skimmed milk and low-fat cheese.

EASY: *ready in 30 minutes*

SERVES 4

275 g/9 oz dried tagliatelle or other ribbon pasta

2 tbsp oil, plus a little extra

500 g/1 lb skinless, boneless chicken breast, cut in bite-size pieces

1 small onion, chopped

250 g/8 oz mushrooms, sliced

125 ml/4 fl oz dry white wine

250 ml/8 fl oz milk

2 tsp plain flour

75 g/3 oz garlic-flavoured Boursin or other cream cheese spread

2 tbsp chopped fresh parsley

salt and pepper

❶ Cook the pasta in plenty of boiling water, then drain.

❷ Meanwhile, heat a large frying pan with the oil. Fry the chicken for 4 minutes until cooked. Set the chicken aside and keep warm.

❸ Heat a little more oil in the pan and fry the onion for a minute. Add the mushrooms and fry together for 4 minutes. Add the wine and boil hard for 3 minutes, till the liquid has evaporated (see Tip).

❹ Combine the milk and flour in a bowl and stir well. Add this to the pan and cook for 3 minutes, whisking constantly, until slightly thickened. Add the chicken, cheese, parsley and a good pinch of freshly ground pepper. Reduce the heat and simmer for 3 minutes or until hot through. Serve over the pasta.

T I P 🥄 Two things make reducing liquids easier. A whisk allows you to stop bits catching on the bottom of the pan but still keep the mixture boiling vigorously. And the shallower and wider the pan, the faster you can boil off excess liquid (a frying pan being the quickest of all).

PASTA WITH CABBAGE AND SMOKED HAM

This dish has a wonderful gamey taste about it; although I got the idea from an American magazine I think it might well have something German in its ancestry. Gently cooked cabbage is a favourite vegetable and, though you might not think of combining it with pasta, the two textures rub along together beautifully.

EASY: *allow 45 minutes; leftovers are delicious reheated*

SERVES 4

4 slices of bacon	250 g/8 oz smoked ham, cut in strips
3 tbsp oil	375 g/12 oz fusilli or other chunky
1 kg/2 lb onions, sliced thinly	pasta
½ tsp caraway or fennel seeds	50 g/2 oz parmesan cheese, grated
¼ small white or savoy cabbage,	125 ml/4 fl oz hot stock (if necessary
core removed, sliced thinly	– see step 4)

❶ Cook the bacon in a large frying pan until brown and crisp. Transfer to a paper towel to drain and then crumble.

❷ Add the oil to the fat in the pan and add the onions and caraway or fennel seeds; turn heat to low and sauté gently until the onions are a deliciously caramelised dark brown – about 25 minutes. Add the cabbage and ham and cook until the cabbage wilts – about 8 minutes.

❸ Meanwhile, cook the pasta in salted, boiling water according to pack instructions; when cooked, drain and return to the pot to keep warm, if necessary.

❹ Add the bacon, onion mixture and cheese to the pasta and toss well over a medium heat, adding stock to moisten if dry.

SALMONBURGERS

Here is a brilliant way to enjoy simple salmon – once a luxury, now the stuff of a quick everyday supper.

FUN TO MAKE: *allow 40 minutes; freezes well*

SERVES 5

125 ml/4 fl oz low-fat mayonnaise	2 tbsp chopped onion
juice of 1 lemon	2 tbsp Dijon mustard
1 garlic clove, crushed	5 × 125 g/4 oz salmon fillets
125 g/4 oz breadcrumbs, dry	a little olive oil
or fresh	5 sesame hamburger buns,
50 ml/2 fl oz milk	toasted

❶ Combine the mayo, 2 tbsp of the lemon juice and garlic in a small serving bowl. Heat the grill and oil the grill pan.

❷ Put the breadcrumbs in a shallow dish. Combine the rest of the lemon juice, milk, onion and mustard in a bowl.

❸ Dip a fish fillet in the milk mixture, then dredge in breadcrumbs. Repeat with the remaining fillets.

❹ Grill for 7 minutes per side, until the fish flakes easily when tested with a fork. When ready, put on half a bun, top with a dollop of mayo mixture and cover with the other half of bun.

TIPS If you prefer, you can make this recipe with fresh tuna. Canned salmon, which is extremely rich in calcium because you tend to eat the bones as well, does not work for this recipe, and nor does canned tuna.

If you wish you can barbecue these burgers, or shallow-fry them in a little oil.

SIMPLE ACCOMPANIMENTS AND SALADS

The theme of this chapter is 'fresh and seasonal' and you'll find in it ideas that make the most of our vegetables as they come in and out of the shops. I am fanatical about shopping with the seasons – rather than blandly reaching for what is put in front of you by the stores and supermarkets, which all too often ignores what is actually being grown in our countryside.

The way to avoid falling for second-rate imports is to always check where produce comes from and, if it looks ropy, substitute something else. The greatest cook in the world can't make delicious food from tired or stale ingredients, and the mere beginner can make something perfect just by shopping for the best.

ALLEGRA'S FATTOUSH TOMATOES

This recipe was invented by London chef Allegra McEvedy. It is simple but extremely useful for entertaining and you'll find her original in her excellent book called The Good Cook *(Hodder and Stoughton, £14.99, ISBN 0 340 767 928). Call the Express Bookshop on 0870 366 6092.* EASY: *allow 20 minutes (make ahead)*

SERVES 4 BUT PEOPLE TEND TO EAT SECONDS!

50 g/2 oz caster sugar	3 sprigs of fresh rosemary
2 tbsp water	8–12 garlic cloves, peeled
75 ml/2½ fl oz extra-virgin olive oil	500 g/1 lb cherry tomatoes
	salt and pepper

❶ Dissolve the sugar in the water and then add the oil, rosemary and garlic. Cook for 5 minutes to infuse – no longer or the rosemary will go a dingy colour. Swirl the pan regularly. Season.

❷ When the garlic is nearly cooked – poke it with a sharp knife and it should be nearly tender – throw in the tomatoes. Roll them around, then cover with a lid and leave for about 2 minutes. Remove from heat just as the tomatoes start to pop. Let them cool to room temperature in the cooking liquor. Serve with half the liquor – see Tip for ideas for the rest. Great with fish or any cold dishes.

T I P 🥣 You will be left with some delicious tomato-oil liquor. Do not waste this precious substance. Allegra suggests you use it in stir-fries, for roasting veg, or in vinaigrettes. It keeps well in the fridge and adds panache to anything.

SOUFFLÉD POTATO CRISPS

*The most fascinating potato dish in the world – every cook should
make this once in their lifetime. Of all my recipes over the years,
this is the one that has required most testing to get it right, and it
is dedicated to my grandfather, who, as a treat, used to make fresh
potato crisps for me and my brother when we went to stay. My
grandfather was a very remarkable man, a spycatcher by profession
(in the immediate postwar years his exploits were much reported by
the* Evening Standard*). I am indebted also to Alex Mackay, formerly
of the Manoir Aux Quat' Saisons in Oxfordshire and now at Le Baou
d'Infer in Provence, for providing an emergency helpline when I
needed it.*

A CHALLENGE: *allow 45 minutes*

SERVES 4 AS AN APPETISER OR ACCOMPANIMENT

**2 Maris Piper potatoes,
    not too big**

**2 litres/3½ pints groundnut oil,
    for deep-frying**

sea salt, to serve

❶ Peel and slice the potatoes across the shorter side into 3 mm/⅛-inch
slices – a mandolin does this well. Wash in two changes of water and dry
on kitchen paper. Put the oil in two deep pans. Heat one to 140°C, the
other to 185°C. Put 8 slices at a time into the cooler oil, stirring often,
and cook for 4–5 minutes, by which time some (but alas not all) slices
will begin to blister, some slightly, some a lot.

❷ As this happens, transfer each slice to the hotter oil. When they are
brown and crisp all over (2–4 minutes), lift out with a slotted spoon and
serve sprinkled with salt.

BEAN AND FETA SALAD

One of the things that makes a good cook exceptional, in my opinion, is an awareness of the seasons, and choosing which recipes to make just when the ingredients are at their best and freshest. Don't even think of making this with those dull imported beans you can buy in sad-looking little packets all year round – better in fact to use frozen (see Tip).

VERY EASY: *allow about 20 minutes*

SERVES 2 OR 4 AS A SIDE DISH

400 g/14 oz green beans

½ medium red onion, sliced finely

25 g/1 oz flaked almonds, toasted

125 g/4 oz feta cheese, cut in dice

For the dressing:

1 garlic clove, chopped finely

3 tbsp raspberry or other vinegar

2 large pinches of salt

100 ml/3½ fl oz olive oil

1 tbsp chopped fresh mint

salt and freshly ground black pepper

❶ Top and tail the beans and cook them in lightly salted water for 3–5 minutes, till just tender to the bite. Drain and put them in cold water to stop them cooking further and fix the colour (otherwise they will turn a dull green).

❷ Make the dressing by mixing garlic, vinegar, salt and pepper. Beat in the olive oil and add the mint.

❸ Pour the dressing over the drained beans, then stir in the onion, almonds and feta cheese. A simple first course or good with fish or chicken dishes.

T I P You can also make this salad with frozen beans – they will need minimal cooking in step 1. Though they are excellent in their way, you won't get quite the crunch of fresh, which is why I urge you to make this in summer using fresh beans.

GREEN BEAN TAPENADE

Here is an inventive treatment for summer's green beans. If you grow them you will know how many you can suddenly have to deal with, and this recipe is just one idea.

Of course another way of dealing with the glut is to freeze them. Plunge them for just a minute or two in fast-boiling water, drain and cool quickly in lots of cold water to fix the colour, before open-freezing; then transfer to bags. Most freezers nowadays have a quick-freeze option, which is ideal for this operation but you do have to remember to activate it an hour or two before the freezing begins.

EASY: *allow 15 minutes*

SERVES 4

500 g/1 lb green beans
75 g/3 oz tapenade
 (black-olive paste)

1 garlic clove, chopped finely
3 tbsp coarsely chopped fresh parsley
2 tsp extra-virgin olive oil

❶ Bring a large saucepan of salted water to the boil. Plunge in the beans and cook for 2–3 minutes, till bright green and just tender. Drain and rinse in lots of cold water to stop cooking and fix the colour. Trim the ends off the beans and slice in half lengthways.

❷ Transfer to a bowl and mix with other ingredients: serve hot or warm.

T I P 🥣 Tapenade is simply black-olive paste – it looks a bit like black pesto. You can buy it in small jars in delicatessens and supermarkets. Leftovers are great stirred into pasta.

CARAMELISED ONION PILAFF

*This is a lovely light accompaniment to meat dishes, specially barbecues.
It does need a little attention while being cooked but I find with outdoor
eating there are so many small preparations to be done, and so very
many things to be taken outside, that you're popping in and out of the
kitchen in any case.*

EASY: *10 minutes to prepare, 45 minutes to cook*

SERVES 6

2 tbsp extra-virgin olive oil

2 large onions, sliced thinly

a pinch of caster sugar

300 g/10 oz rice, preferably basmati,
   washed if directed on packet

750 ml/1¼ pints chicken stock

3 tbsp grated parmesan cheese

2 tbsp snipped fresh chives

salt and pepper

❶ Combine the oil, onions, sugar and a good pinch of salt in a large,
heavy pan and cook over a moderate heat, stirring often, till soft – about
5 minutes. Reduce heat to low and cook, half-covered with the saucepan
lid, for about 20 minutes, by which time the onion should be browned.
This cooking method brings out the natural sweetness of the onions and
cannot be rushed.

❷ Stir in the rice and stock. Bring the boil, season with salt and pepper
and simmer covered for 15–20 minutes, till the rice is tender.

❸ Stir in the parmesan, transfer to a serving dish and sprinkle with
chives. Serve at once.

> **TIP** 🥣 Extra-virgin olive oil, which is the *crème de la crème*
> of olive oils, is only worth using when its olivey, often slightly bitter
> flavour enhances the finished dish. I do not use it on other occasions,
> as it is can be a shocking price.

NEW POTATOES WITH CHIMICHURRI SAUCE

Chimichurri is a herby South American flavouring, often used in barbecue and pork recipes. Although this recipe has a lot of ingredients, there is nothing out of the ordinary to buy and it is deliciously different.

HARDLY ANY COOKING: *allow 1¹/₂ hours*

SERVES 4

1 packet of halloumi cheese (see Tip)

625 g/1¹/₄ lb new potatoes

sea salt

For the marinade:

50 ml/2 fl oz olive oil

1 garlic clove, crushed

¹/₂ tsp freshly grated ginger

1 spring onion, chopped

1 red chilli, de-seeded and
   chopped finely

1 tbsp mild red-wine vinegar

4 tbsp water

2 tbsp corn oil

For the chimichurri sauce:

1 tbsp finely chopped fresh rosemary

2 tbsp finely chopped fresh thyme

2 tbsp finely chopped fresh oregano

2 tbsp finely chopped fresh sage

5 tbsp finely chopped fresh parsley

1 tsp grated lime zest

1 tsp salt

freshly ground black pepper

a pinch of sugar

75 ml/2¹/₂ fl oz olive oil

❶ Slice the cheese. Combine the marinade ingredients and mix with the cheese. Leave for at least an hour, or overnight.

❷ Put all the sauce ingredients, except the oil, in a blender and work to a rough paste. Remove from processor and beat in the oil.

❸ Boil the potatoes till tender, drain and sprinkle with salt.

❹ Lightly fry the halloumi cheese in its marinade for about 5 minutes. Mix with the hot potatoes and pour over the cold sauce.

> **T I P** 🥄 Halloumi is a dense, mildly salted cheese from Cyprus, which can be made from cow's, sheep's or goat's milk. It is a bit like tough mozzarella, and stands up well to frying. The first time I ever ate it it had been grilled till golden – rather like thick cheese crisps.

POTATO AND LEEK GRATIN

For a melt-in-the-mouth result go for proper old potatoes, Maris Piper or King Edward.

QUICK AND EASY: *20 minutes to prepare, 1¹/4 hours in the oven*

SERVES 6

125 ml/4 fl oz stock

142 ml carton of double cream

150 ml/¹/4 pint milk

1 garlic clove, crushed

1 bay leaf

1.05 kg/2¹/4 lb potatoes, peeled and
  sliced thinly

1 large leek, washed well and
  sliced thinly

175 g/6 oz sliced ham, chopped

75 g/3 oz cheese, grated

salt, pepper and freshly ground
  nutmeg

❶ Put the first five ingredients in a small saucepan, bring to the boil, draw off the heat and leave to infuse as you continue preparing the dish.

❷ Preheat the oven to 180°C/170°C fan oven/Gas Mark 4. Butter a 2.25-litre/4-pint gratin dish thoroughly. Spread about a third of the potatoes on the bottom, season with salt, pepper and nutmeg. Lay on top half the leeks and half the ham. Repeat, seasoning the potatoes as before. Finish with the last lot of potatoes on top. Season once more.

❸ Pour over the flavoured cream, discarding the garlic if you wish. Tuck the bay leaf in the middle of the dish. Sprinkle with the cheese. Stand on a baking tray in case it boils over.

❹ Bake, loosely covered with foil, for 30 minutes. Test the potatoes with a knife – they should be beginning to go tender. Remove the foil and bake for 35–45 minutes more, basting occasionally with the creamy juices, until the potatoes are meltingly tender. Leave to cool for 15 minutes before serving. Excellent with a tomato salad.

TIP 🥄 The sauce slightly separates – a characteristic of the dish and it's none the less delicious for it.

FENNEL À LA GRECQUE

This dish is the product of something of a tangle of nationalities. A la grecque refers to the Greek style of the dish – onions, tomato, spices (in particular coriander) and sultanas. The recipe was passed to me by an Irish friend, Fiona McCowan who in turn procured it some years ago from a Canadian called Henry.

A recipe that is so begged and borrowed obviously has a lot going for it.

EASY: *allow 1 hour*

SERVES 2–3 AS A MAIN COURSE,
4 AS AN ACCOMPANIMENT

4 tbsp olive oil

2 heads of fennel, trimmed and
quartered

200 g/7 oz small onions, such as
pickling onions or shallots (see Tip)

½ tsp salt

½ tsp ground white pepper

½ tsp cayenne pepper (or less if
you don't like hot food)

½ tsp ground coriander

½ tsp chopped fresh thyme or
¼ tsp dried thyme

2 tbsp tomato purée

75 ml/3 fl oz dry white wine

1 bay leaf

50 g/2 oz sultanas or raisins

❶ Take a medium casserole and heat the oil. Fry the fennel and onions for 4–5 minutes, then add everything except the sultanas or raisins.

❷ Cover the pan and simmer for 15 minutes, then add the sultanas or raisins. Simmer for 15 minutes longer or until the fennel and onions are tender and then serve hot or cold.

TIP 🥄 If the onions are very small it can be an almighty fiddle to peel them. What helps is to put them in a bowl and pour boiling water over; leave for 2–3 minutes and then the skins should pop off.

GRILLED MEDITERRANEAN POTATO SALAD

Here is a very tasty Mediterranean-style salad, spiced up by peppers, anchovies, capers and olives. It is packed with flavour, and will eclipse the delicate flavours of fish or chicken, so serve with barbecued or other tasty fare.

EASY: *allow 50 minutes, including 40 minutes roasting*

SERVES 6, AS A SIDE DISH

1 kg/2 lb medium potatoes, peeled and sliced thinly

2 tbsp olive oil

½ tsp sea salt

1 jar of antipasto peppers, drained

2 tbsp capers, drained and rinsed

a good handful of black olives, pitted

3 tbsp roughly chopped fresh parsley

For the dressing:

4 anchovy fillets

3 tbsp red-wine vinegar

½ tsp sea salt

freshly ground black pepper

2 tbsp olive oil

❶ Preheat the oven to 220°C/200°C fan oven/Gas Mark 7. In a bowl, combine the potatoes, olive oil and salt. Roast the potatoes on a baking tray for 40 minutes, till nicely browned, turning halfway through.

❷ Make the dressing: finely chop the anchovy fillets, add the vinegar, salt and a few turns of pepper. Whisk in the oil.

❸ Mix the potatoes, drained peppers, capers, olives and parsley, toss with the dressing and serve warm or cold.

TIP 🥄 Jars of antipasto-style peppers are a boon, and save messing round grilling pepper and trying to peel off the burnt bits of skin – an operation that drives me quickly to distraction.

JANSSEN'S TEMPTATION

Swedish cooking, like Swedish ingredients, is not well understood in this country: there is much more to it than herrings and smorgasbords. I reckon that Swedish food, like Swedish style, is likely to be one of the big stories over the next couple of years. This dish is the national favourite way of serving potatoes.

EASY: *allow 1 hour 10 minutes*

SERVES 6–8

900 g/2 lb potatoes

50 g/2 oz butter

2 large onions, sliced

2 cans of anchovies in oil – preferably
   Swedish, drained (see Tip)

200 ml/7 fl oz double cream

100 ml/3½ fl oz milk

pepper

❶ Preheat the oven to 220°C/200°C fan oven/Gas Mark 7. Peel and slice the potatoes thinly and leave in cold water till ready to cook. Use a little of the butter to grease a 1.7-litre/3-pint ovenproof dish.

❷ Sauté the onions gently in half the butter till slightly softened, but not coloured – about 5 minutes. Drain the potatoes and dry well. Arrange half in the casserole, then add half the onion, seasoning the layers with pepper (not salt) as you go. Add the anchovies, chopped, then cover with the remaining onion and potatoes. Put the remaining butter on top of the potatoes.

❸ Heat the cream and milk to boiling and then pour over the potatoes. Bake for 20 minutes. Then reduce the heat to 180°C/160°C fan oven/Gas Mark 4 for a further 20–30 minutes, till the potatoes are tender.

T I P The anchovy taste is not pronounced – if you wish, drizzle some of the anchovy oil over the onions too.

PARSNIPS MOLLY PARKIN

I long wondered about the name of this baked vegetable dish; Molly Parkin is a legendary personality, originally a fashion journalist and in recent years a partygoer and (if she will forgive my saying it) society eccentric.

In the end, I took my courage in my hands, found out Molly's telephone number and asked her to tell me how the dish had come about. She remembers it fondly. 'Well, you see,' she starts, 'I was very friendly with a wonderful cook called Denis Curtis' (long-time cookery writer of the Sunday Telegraph*). 'We both came from the Welsh hills and used to talk about our grannies. I remember going down to his house in Bray and he did something amazing with pineapple – it was like a Meccano sculpture. I told Denis how much I hated vegetables, unless they were cooked to a pulp and served with lots of gravy.'*

'One day someone rang up and said have you seen Denis's recipe this week? He'd made up this dish and dedicated it to me, out of mischief. It's absolutely gorgeous! He had to be a genius to make parsnips palatable to me.'

DELICIOUSLY DIFFERENT: *40 minutes to prepare, 40 minutes to cook*

SERVES 4, AS A MAIN COURSE

4 tbsp oil

1 onion, sliced thinly

1 garlic clove, chopped

875 g/1¾ lb parsnips, peeled, cored if tough and sliced thinly

400 g/14 oz tomatoes

50 g/2 oz butter

3 tbsp demerara or other brown sugar

284 ml carton of single or whipping cream

75 g/3 oz Cheddar cheese, grated

3 tbsp fresh white breadcrumbs

salt and pepper

❶ Preheat the oven to 160°C/140°C fan oven/Gas Mark 3. Heat the oil and fry the onion for about 6 minutes, till tender and just turning golden, adding garlic a couple of minutes before the end. Boil the parsnips in salted water till completely tender. Pour boiling water over the tomatoes, leave for a minute and then fish them out and remove their skins. Slice roughly and discard seeds and pulp.

❷ Grease a 1.2-litre/2-pint ovenproof dish with half the butter. Put one-third of the parsnips in the base, season well with salt, pepper and 1 tbsp of the sugar and pour over one-third of the cream. Now put half the tomatoes and onion-garlic mixture on top. Repeat with another layer of parsnips and cream, then tomatoes and onions, then the remaining parsnips and cream, so that you have parsnips on top. Sprinkle with the cheese, then dot with the remaining butter and scatter the breadcrumbs on top.

❸ Bake for 40 minutes until golden.

T I P 🥣 Parsnips are reputed to be sweeter when the frost has nipped them. I also find they taste much better – and are easier to peel – if you keep them in the salad drawer of the fridge. Perhaps this acts as a mild frosting in itself?

PESTO NEW POTATOES

Having been brought up in the island of Jersey, I know how delicious a freshly dug Jersey Royal can be. Here is an easy idea for new potatoes, with ideas to vary it.

EASY: *allow 30 minutes*

SERVES 4, AS AN ACCOMPANIMENT

550 g/1 lb 2 oz new potatoes,
    scrubbed and halved or
    quartered if large

2–3 tsp pesto
25 g/1 oz parmesan cheese, grated
salt and pepper

❶ Boil the potatoes in simmering water till tender. Do not remove them too soon – they do need to be fully cooked. Drain and allow to cool.

❷ Toss in the pesto, season to taste and serve, dusted with the parmesan.

VARIATIONS 🥣 You can also make a Moroccan Potato Salad. Harissa paste is an extremely hot Moroccan chilli paste that you will find in tubes, small cans or jars in delicatessens or good supermarkets (including Sainsbury's). Until you are used to it, use in very small quantities! Substitute 1 tsp of harissa paste, mixed with 1 tbsp of olive oil, for the pesto and garnish with chopped mint instead of the parmesan. Serve hot or cold.

Or you can whip up a New Potato And Onion Salad. Substitute 1–2 tbsp of balsamic vinegar for the pesto, plus half a red onion, very finely chopped. Garnish with fresh thyme leaves. Serve hot or cold.

PERFECT GARLIC MASH

Mashed potato has become wildly fashionable over the last couple of years, and every top chef gives it his own signature. This recipe looks quite over the top, with masses of garlic and a good whack of butter, but there is nothing more delicious.

If you are the proud owner of a potato ricer, this will give you the best texture. Otherwise, an ordinary masher will do the trick. Whatever you do, don't even think about the food processor, which will turn your efforts into wallpaper paste.

EASY: *ready in under an hour*

SERVES 4 – 6

2 heads of garlic, cloves separated but not peeled	**125 g/4 oz butter**
	250 ml/8 fl oz single cream, warmed
1 kg/2 lb potatoes, peeled	**1½ tsp salt**

❶ Toast the garlic by putting it in a small frying pan and heating over the lowest possible heat, shaking the pan often, until the cloves are dark brown – about 20 minutes. Leave for 15–20 minutes and check the insides are soft. Discard the skins and mash the garlic to a paste with a fork.

❷ Cook the potatoes in plenty of salted water and until tender, about 20–30 minutes. Drain and mash thoroughly, then put through a ricer or mouli if you have one, back into the saucepan. Stir in butter with a wooden spoon, then lightly whisk in the cream and seasoning. Serve at once.

VARIATION If you wish, stir in 125 g/4 oz of grated Cheddar when you add the cream, then heat gently till the cheese has melted.

SMOKED SALMON AND LENTIL SALAD

This is a most unusual and delectable salad to serve as a first course – an adventure in texture as well as flavour. Although on the fancy side it requires no cooking skills, the only fiddly part being arranging it on the plates. I like cooking lentils – no need to presoak – but if you are in a rush you can use canned ones; if so, you do not need a whole tin, just 125 g/4 oz. This recipe is unstinting with the smoked salmon; if you wish you can use a smaller amount, or pieces, though the effect will obviously be less lavish.

EASY AND SPECIAL: *30 minutes to prepare, 25–30 minutes to cook*

SERVES 4

For the lentils:

50 g/2 oz green lentils (preferably Puy lentils – see Tip)

600 ml/1 pint in total of white wine, dry or medium, and water, mixed

2 slices of bacon, fried till crisp and cooled, then crumbled

1 shallot or two spring onions, chopped finely

250 g/8 oz smoked salmon, sliced thinly then cut in large strips about 10 × 5 cm/4 × 2 inches

a handful of fresh dill, chopped finely, plus a few sprigs for garnish

a bag of mixed salad leaves

4 tbsp soured cream

4 fresh dill sprigs, to garnish

For the dressing:

2 tsp Dijon mustard

2 tbsp white-wine vinegar

4 tbsp walnut oil

salt and pepper

❶ Cook the lentils: wash well (no need to soak) then put in a pan with the wine and water and salt (not too much on account of the smoked salmon). Bring to the boil and boil for 20–25 minutes, till tender but not falling to bits. Lentils vary so do check. Drain and cool.

❷ To make the dressing, whisk the mustard and vinegar, then whisk in the walnut oil gradually till thickened and emulsified. Season well.

3 Mix the lentils with the bacon, the shallots or spring onions and one-third of the dressing. Fold in the salmon and the chopped dill.

4 Toss the salad leaves in a bowl with half the remaining dressing.

5 Assembly time: take four plates. Put the salmon-lentil mixture on one half of each plate and drizzle over a little of the remaining dressing. Put the salad leaves on the other half of the plate. Put a line of soured cream between the two. Garnish with a dill sprig and serve.

T I P 🥣 Puy lentils are a specially tender, tiny and aristocratic sort of lentil from France. Look out for them but if you can't find them, choose continental lentils or, failing these, green ones.

SPECIAL FRIED RICE

*If you love the fried rice they do in Chinese restaurants you can make
something ten times as tasty and exciting at home. Make sure you have
everything ready before you start, chopped and laid out on boards in
running order (imagine you're a TV cook).*

FUN TO MAKE: *allow 30 minutes (but get the rice cooked an hour ahead)*

SERVES 4 – 6

50 ml/2 fl oz oyster sauce
   (from Chinese shops)

1 tbsp soy sauce (I like Kikkoman
   best)

3 tbsp sunflower oil

2 large eggs, lightly beaten

150 g/5 oz frozen peas or petits
   pois, thawed

2 medium garlic cloves, chopped

625 g/1¼ lb cooked, cooled
   long-grain rice (300 g/10 oz
   uncooked weight)

65 g/2½ oz beansprouts

5 spring onions, sliced thinly

❶ Combine the oyster and soy sauces in a small bowl and set aside.

❷ Heat a large, non-stick frying pan and, when hot, add 1½ tsp of the
oil. Swirl to coat the bottom of the pan. Add the eggs and cook without
stirring for 20 seconds, until they just begin to set, then scramble and
break up for 1 minute longer. Set aside.

❸ Return the pan to the heat and add the remaining oil. Now add the
ingredients as follows, stirring all the time: add the peas and cook for
30 seconds. Add the garlic and cook for 30 seconds. Add the rice and
oyster sauce mix and cook for 3 minutes. Add the eggs, beansprouts
and spring onions and cook for 1 minute.

❹ Now serve!

SWEDISH BLUE CHEESE SALAD

This salad has a light dressing that in Sweden is made with Swedish cheese, but here Danish blue or any crumbly British blue will do.

EASY AND SPECIAL: *allow 30 minutes, excellent with salmon*

SERVES 4

1 tbsp olive oil

12 asparagus spears (optional), trimmed and sliced into 2.5 cm/ 1-inch pieces

1 small lettuce, preferably cos, torn up

6 small new potatoes, cooked and sliced

1 small red onion, sliced thinly

1 British apple, cored and sliced

For the croûtons:

2 slices of white bread

1 tbsp butter

For the blue cheese dressing:

50 g/2 oz blue cheese

4 tbsp Greek yogurt

1 tbsp milk

❶ Make the croûtons by frying the bread, cut in small cubes, in the butter for 5 minutes, turning often.

❷ Heat the oil and fry the asparagus pieces, if using, until just tender. Put them in the bottom of a large salad bowl, preferably glass. Sweden is famed for its modern glass and, if you are the owner of a beautiful Orrefors bowl, now is the time to put it to proud use. Layer the lettuce, potatoes, onion and apple in the bowl.

❸ Whisk the dressing ingredients till frothy and pour over the salad. Sprinkle the croûtons on top and then toss the salad at the table.

T I P 🥣 Sweden prides itself on the crisp freshness of its vegetables, as visits to the Arsta wholesale market and Ostermalmshallen foodmarket in Sweden proved to me when I visited to experience the local cuisine. Ranks of gleaming vegetables, including some amazing organically grown herbs I have never seen before, make you long to eat them as quickly and crunchily as possible.

BROAD BEAN SALAD
WITH PROSCIUTTO

Many people – cooks included – dislike broad beans, but I think if they could taste a bean freshly podded from the garden they might change their minds. Squeaky fresh and jade green, this is a vegetable that has to be enjoyed fresh – and the sad, flaccid pods you find in many supermarkets must have been knocking around for days.

In fact, if you can't find good fresh beans, I would recommend frozen – which have the benefit that they are tender, young and frozen within hours of being picked. If using frozen for this recipe, cook them briefly first, then cool.

EASY: *allow 30 minutes*

AN EASY STARTER FOR 6

3 tbsp olive oil

leaves of a sprig of fresh rosemary, chopped roughly

1.5 kg/3½ lb fresh broad beans (weight before podding) or about 500 g/1 lb podded broad beans

2 spring onions, sliced finely

12 slices of prosciutto (or two 185 g packets), cut in large strips

salt and pepper

❶ Gently heat the oil in a pan with the rosemary, then set aside to infuse.

❷ Cook the beans in fast-boiling, salted water till just tender (about 8–10 minutes), then drain and transfer to a serving bowl.

❸ Add the oil and rosemary and toss until coated. Mix in the spring onions and ham, then season. Serve at room temperature.

> **T I P** 🥄 Prosciutto is one of many continental cooked hams available in delis and supermarkets now. If you can find Spanish ham it makes a delicious, slightly spicy alternative.

simple accompaniments and salads

chapter 4

EXCITING VEGETARIAN

DISHES

More and more of the time I enjoy meat-free meals. It is not just that I like the idea of enjoying vegetables but, as often as not, it is inconvenient to have meat or fish around. They are demanding ingredients, and you have to cook them whether you fancy them or not; whereas vegetables – though of course best eaten fresh – are much more accommodating. Vegetarian food has come a long way from its rather earnest beginnings, and I hope vegetarians and meat-eaters alike will find these dishes tasty and satisfying for suppers and lunches.

MACARONI CHEESE
WITH A DIFFERENCE

You can adapt the recipe according to the vegetables you have available, and make it even more jazzy by adding peppers of different colours. Although they look so distinctive, the green, red, orange and yellow peppers you can find nowadays in markets and supermarkets do not really taste so different when you get down to it, so I tend to employ them according to their cosmetic effect.

WORTH THE TROUBLE: *35 minutes to prepare, 20 minutes to bake; freezes well*

SERVES 6

For the vegetables:

2 tbsp olive oil

1 onion, sliced thinly

1 garlic clove, crushed

4 small peppers, sliced thinly

**4 small courgettes, halved
   lengthways and sliced thinly**

**250 g/8 oz dried pasta shapes,
   such as macaroni or penne**

For the sauce:

40 g/1½ oz butter

3 tbsp plain flour

**a handful of fresh herb sprigs, such
   as rosemary, sage, bay leaves**

600 ml/1 pint milk

175 g/6 oz Cheddar cheese, grated

salt and pepper

❶ Heat half the oil. Fry the onion for 5 minutes, till tender but not brown. Add the garlic and peppers and fry for 3 minutes, then add the courgettes and cook for 3 minutes longer, adding the remaining oil if necessary. Season well and set aside.

❷ Cook the pasta in lots of salted water till just done – do not overcook as the dish is finished in the oven. When cooked, drain not too thoroughly and return to the saucepan. Add the vegetables and mix well.

❸ Make the sauce: heat the butter in a medium pan and keep heating until it starts to colour and goes a deep nut brown – emitting a wonderful nutty aroma as it does so. This takes 3–5 minutes – it may sputter a bit in the pan but this is normal. Once it is a good colour, but not actually blackened, stir in the flour and herbs. Cook for 2–3 minutes till well combined (the mixture will look a strange grey colour) and then gradually add the milk, ensuring each addition is smoothly combined before continuing with the next. The sauce should be the consistency of single cream. Pour over the vegetable and pasta mixture, add three-quarters of the cheese, combine well and check it is well seasoned. Transfer to a large shallow ovenproof dish, no need to grease, and sprinkle the remaining cheese on top.

❹ So much can be done well in advance. To finish the dish, preheat the oven to 200°C/180°C fan oven/Gas Mark 6 and bake for 20 minutes till browned. Serve with a salad.

T I P I have found a new way to prepare peppers. Slice each end off thinly and discard the stem, which will pop out obligingly. You now have a cylinder a bit like a miniature oil drum. Make a slit right down one side with a small knife, then work your knife round the inside of the pepper, slicing off the membrane and seeds in one. Quick and neat once you get the hang of this.

BAKED CINNAMON
RATATOUILLE PIES

Here is a flavourful recipe for ratatouille that makes a popular main course for vegetarians, served as a puff pastry pie.

WORTH THE TROUBLE: *allow 1 hour but make the ratatouille ahead; can be frozen before baking*

SERVES 8

1 aubergine, sliced, sprinkled
   with salt, left for an hour then
   washed and patted dry
1 small courgette
1 onion
3 tbsp olive oil
1 garlic clove
2 × 400 g cans of chopped tomatoes

grated zest of 1 orange
½ tsp ground cinnamon
1 tbsp finely chopped fresh ginger
1½ tsp salt and plenty of pepper
425 g packet of ready-rolled
   puff pastry
beaten egg, for brushing the pastry

❶ Dice the aubergine and courgette. Chop the onion, heat the oil and fry the onion, aubergine and courgette for about 7 minutes, till golden. Crush the garlic clove and add to the pan.

❷ Add the tomatoes, orange zest, cinnamon, ginger, salt and pepper and simmer gently, covered, for 30–40 minutes. Allow to cool – if you make it a day ahead you will find it tastes even better.

❸ Preheat the oven to 220°C/225°C fan oven/Gas Mark 6. Dig out eight small ramekins, or larger ones if serving as a main course. Cut out eight circles from the pastry, using a ramekin as a cutter, then spoon the ratatouille into the ramekins till nearly full. Press a lid of pastry on to each dish.

❹ Brush the pastry with the egg and make a small slit. Decorate with bits of pastry if you wish.

❺ Bake for 12–15 minutes (longer if you are using larger dishes) and serve hot.

BARLEY 'RISOTTO'

I am a great fan of pearl barley, but it is hardly called for in every recipe and a box or bag of it tends to sit forever at the back of your storecupboard. Instead of just tossing a handful into home-made soups, try this idea based on the pilaff or risotto principle, in which barley is simmered in stock and then served quite simply with a little pesto folded through.

A CINCH: *allow 45 minutes*

SERVES 4 AS A MAIN COURSE WITH A SALAD, 6 AS A SIDE DISH

2 tbsp oil

1 onion, chopped

200 g/7 oz pearl barley, rinsed
   well and drained

1 bay leaf

900 ml/1½ pints vegetable stock

½ tsp salt and plenty of freshly
   ground black pepper

2 tbsp ready-made pesto

1 Heat the oil in a large casserole and gently cook the onion for about 7 minutes, till soft but not golden. Stir in the barley, bay leaf, stock and seasoning.

2 Bring to a boil, then cover and simmer for 30 minutes.

3 Remove from the heat, allow to stand for 5 minutes uncovered, then fold in the pesto and serve.

T I P On the subject of pearl barley, look out in your health food shop (such as Holland and Barrett) for a mixture of dried grains and vegetables called soup or broth mix. These are ideal to bulk up a simple soup and turn it into something substantial and nutritious.

CANNELLINI BEAN SALAD

Canned beans and pulses are one of the great foods of our day. The whole family loves them and they are filled with protein; you don't even have to cook them. Many recipes nowadays suggest taking a tin of beans, draining it and puréeing in a blender or processor with garlic and perhaps other flavourings to make a bean mash. This is quite wonderful hot or cold, and can be mixed with potato to make the nicest mash you ever tasted. In this recipe, which is also ideal for vegetarians, exciting flavours, textures and colours make a brilliant supper dish.

NO COOKING: *allow 10 minutes*

SERVES 4

1 small red onion	**½ iceburg or 1 cos lettuce**
1 small red or yellow pepper	**250 g pack of feta cheese**
400 g can of cannellini beans	**freshly ground black pepper**
4 tbsp ready-made vinaigrette	**warm Italian bread, to serve**

❶ Finely slice the onion and pepper. Cut each pepper slice in half. Drain and rinse the beans. Put these ingredients in a salad bowl, add the dressing and mix well.

❷ Tear the lettuce leaves straight into the bowl. Break the feta into chunks, throw into the salad and season with black pepper. Serve with warm Italian bread.

T I P 🥄 If you can't find cannellini beans almost any other sort will do. The same goes for feta cheese: if you can't find any (it's sometimes sold in oil in jars) then use Lancashire or another white, crumbly cheese.

CLASSIC GENOESE PASTA

This recipe is Genoa's favourite dish, and the recipe is based on one in an excellent new book, Pasta – Every Way for Every Day *by Eric Treuille and Anna Del Conte (Dorling Kindersley, £12.99; call the Express Bookshop on 0870 366 6092). If you can find* trofie – *small pasta twists – these are the authentic choice, otherwise go for linguine or spaghetti.*

QUICK AND EASY: *allow 25 minutes*

SERVES 4 – 6

125 g/4 oz fine green beans, trimmed	**150 g/5 oz pesto**
	a little extra-virgin olive oil
4 small waxy potatoes, sliced thinly	**salt and pepper**
500 g/1 lb dried pasta, such as linguine or spaghetti	

❶ Cook the beans in a large pan of boiling, salted water till just tender – 5 minutes. Remove with a slotted spoon and plunge into cold water. Add the potatoes to the cooking water and cook till tender, about 6–8 minutes. Remove with a slotted spoon.

❷ Still using the same boiling water, cook the pasta until cooked but still slightly firm to the bite. Drain, reserving a little of the cooking water. Return the pasta, beans and potatoes, with the pesto and a glug of oil, to the cooking pot and toss well to warm through, adding the reserved water if it looks dry. Check the seasoning and serve.

T I P 🥄 Pesto is by no means just a summer sauce – in fact it was created as a way to preserve basil through the winter (and on ships sailing out of Genoa). You do, however, want to make this when you can find nice fresh beans.

MEDITERRANEAN VEGETABLE TAGLIOLINI

This dish was inspired by one I ate in a trendy Notting Hill restaurant one lunchtime. Film star Richard E. Grant and his family were eating lunch at the next table, which lent an atmosphere of glamour to the establishment, but what really caught my attention was this exceedingly simple pasta dish.

EASY: *allow 20–30 minutes*

SERVES 4

1 red pepper

2 small courgettes

1 small aubergine

2 garlic cloves

5 tbsp olive oil

250 g pack of fresh tagliolini (see Tip)

salt and freshly ground black pepper

grated parmesan cheese, to serve

❶ Halve and de-seed the pepper, then cut the flesh into small squares. Trim the courgettes and aubergine and cut these into small cubes. Finely chop the garlic.

❷ Heat the olive oil in a frying pan, add the garlic and fry briefly. Add the vegetables and fry over moderate heat for 8–10 minutes, stirring occasionally until the vegetables are softened. Season well with salt and pepper.

❸ Bring a large pan of generously salted water to the boil. Add the pasta and cook for 2 minutes, then drain, reserving a few tablespoons of the cooking water. Return to the pan and add the vegetables, along with the pan juices and reserved cooking water if necessary. Toss well, then serve each portion with freshly grated parmesan and black pepper sprinkled over.

TIP Tagliolini are a thinner version of tagliatelle. If you can't get them, use 400 g/14 oz of tagliatelle and cook for the time recommended on the pack.

MUSHROOM GOULASH

Autumn is the mushroom season and, if you live near the New Forest, you will no doubt be drawn to the early morning mushroom forages that now abound there. This recipe is adapted from a great recipe in a book called Mmm... Mushrooms *(Simon & Schuster, £6.99; call the Express Bookshop on 0870 366 6092) by Victoria Lloyd-Davies.*

NO PROBLEMS: *allow 10 minutes to make, 20 minutes to cook*

SERVES 4, GENEROUSLY

2 tbsp oil

1 large leek, sliced

1 green pepper, de-seeded and cut in small squares

500 g/1 lb closed-cup mushrooms, sliced thickly

175 g/6 oz chestnut mushrooms, halved (see Tip)

2 tbsp paprika

150 ml/½ pint vegetable stock

2 tbsp tomato passata or 2 tsp tomato purée

2 tbsp chopped fresh parsley

salt and pepper

To serve:

550 g/1 lb 2 oz pack of fresh tagliatelle

2 tbsp crème fraîche

1 Heat the oil and gently cook the leek and pepper for 2 minutes; then stir in the mushrooms. Cover and cook gently for 5 minutes, stirring occasionally. Stir in the paprika and cook for a minute. Add the stock, tomato passata or purée and parsley and season to taste. Cook, uncovered, for 10 minutes, stirring occasionally.

2 Meanwhile, cook the pasta. Drain and divide between four plates, then top with the goulash and a dollop of crème fraîche.

T I P 🥣 Chestnut mushrooms are chunky brown mushrooms with a more intense flavour than regular ones. If you can't find them, simply up the quantity of normal mushrooms.

PASTA WITH GARLIC, OIL AND BREADCRUMBS

*Here is one of the Italian classics — so simple, so good, and using plain
storecupboard ingredients. When I was a small child, my father moved
our family to Rome and it is said that Italian was the first language
for me and my brother. It certainly gave us a taste for pasta, and it is
still my quick supper of choice. The best tip of all for wonderful pasta
is to save a little of the pasta cooking water when draining, to thin
the sauce if necessary.*

EASY: *allow 30 minutes*

SERVES 4 – 6

**500 g/1 lb dried spaghetti or
  linguine**

a good knob of butter

25 g/1 oz breadcrumbs

**15 g/½ oz parmesan cheese,
  grated**

3 garlic cloves, crushed

50 ml/2 fl oz extra-virgin olive oil

½ tsp chilli flakes

**50 ml/2 fl oz Martini or other dry
  vermouth**

salt and pepper

❶ Warm a large serving bowl. Cook the pasta in masses of salted, boiling
water, stirring from time to time. Set aside 125 ml/4 fl oz of cooking
water before draining the pasta.

❷ Heat the butter in a large, heavy frying pan and fry the breadcrumbs
till brown and fragrant, about 2–3 minutes. Transfer to a small bowl, with
the cheese and half the garlic. Wipe out the frying pan with kitchen paper.

❸ Mix the remaining garlic with 1 tsp water. Heat the olive oil, garlic
mixture and chilli flakes in the frying pan for 2 minutes. Add the Martini,
reserved cooking water, 1 tsp salt and pepper and cook for a minute.
Toss the pasta and sauce in the bowl and sprinkle with the breadcrumbs
before serving with a fresh salad.

COURGETTES STUFFED WITH CHEDDAR & TOMATOES

Some recipes are best followed to the letter, others are capable of variation. This is one of the latter – you can follow the basic idea but experiment with different vegetables, herbs and cheese.

WORTH THE TROUBLE: *allow 1 hour*

SERVES 4

3 medium potatoes (about 500 g/1 lb), scrubbed and cut in 1 cm/½-inch cubes

4 tbsp olive oil

4 courgettes

1 onion, chopped finely

5 large garlic cloves, chopped finely

3 large tomatoes, de-seeded and chopped

3 tbsp chopped fresh basil leaves

175 g/6 oz Cheddar cheese, grated

salt and pepper

❶ Preheat the oven to 200°C/180°C fan oven/Gas Mark 6. Toss the potatoes with 1 tbsp of the olive oil and seasoning, and spread in a single layer on a baking sheet. Put in the oven and roast for about 15–20 minutes, till tender and lightly browned. Remove from oven.

❷ Meanwhile, halve the courgettes lengthways. With a small spoon, scoop out the seeds and most of the flesh, to leave a thin shell. Season the cut sides and brush with 2 tablespoons of the oil. Put cut-side down on a baking sheet and bake in the oven for about 10 minutes, till slightly softened and wrinkled.

❸ Heat the remaining tbsp of oil in a large frying pan. Add the onion and cook for about 10 minutes over a low heat; add the garlic, the tomatoes and the cooked potatoes and cook for 5 minutes, till heated through. Off the heat, stir in the basil, half the cheese and seasoning.

❹ Divide the filling between the courgettes. Sprinkle lightly with the remaining cheese and bake till heated through and the cheese on top is spotty brown. Serve at once.

MASHED POTATO AND GOAT'S CHEESE GRATIN

I only started cooking with goat's cheese a couple of years ago and it makes a great ingredient – you can toast it, melt it, or as here, mix it with other ingredients and brown it in a hot oven. Although most of the goat's cheese you can buy is French (and very strong) my favourite sort has to be Capricorn, which comes from Somerset: clean, mild and fresh tasting.

NO TROUBLE: *ready in 1 hour 20 minutes*

SERVES 4–6, AS AN ACCOMPANIMENT

1 kg/2 lb potatoes, peeled and cut in chunks

2 large garlic cloves, peeled

75 g/3 oz butter

100 g/3½ soft goat's cheese (such as Capricorn), crumbled

50 ml/2 fl oz whipping cream

50 g/2 oz spring onions, sliced thinly

salt and pepper

❶ Butter a 1.75-litre/3-pint oval baking dish. Put the potatoes and garlic in a large pan of salted water and boil until tender, about 10–15 minutes. Drain and return both potatoes and garlic to the pot.

❷ Meanwhile, heat most of the butter and the cheese and cream in a small saucepan over a low heat till smooth – less than 5 minutes. Set aside.

❸ Mash the potatoes and garlic until smooth, then stir in the goat's cheese mix and the spring onions. Season and transfer to the baking dish. (You can prepare this far in advance, if convenient, up to a day ahead.)

❹ When ready to cook, heat the oven to 200°C/180°C fan oven/Gas Mark 6. Melt the remaining butter and drizzle over the top of the dish. Bake until golden and bubbling round the edges – about 40 minutes. Leave to stand for 10 minutes before serving.

> **TIP** As a good all-purpose potato that won't let you down whatever you choose to do with it, Maris Piper is the choice.

STILTON AND PUMPKIN RISOTTO

Here's a delicious, if rather rich, solution to the problem of what to do with the pumpkin flesh that you scoop out of your Hallowe'en pumpkin: you will need only 250 g/8 oz so, if you haven't got pumpkin, buy another (smaller) member of the squash family, such as butternut squash.

Sage and onion really set off the flavours of this creamy risotto, which is suitable for vegetarians. You will notice from the method that this is not a true risotto, in that the liquid is added all at once, rather than stirred in gradually, but it is excellent nevertheless.

NOT DIFFICULT, BUT YOU DO NEED TO STAND AND STIR: *allow 45 minutes*

SERVES 4

2 tbsp oil	1 litre/1¾ pints vegetable stock,
50 g/2 oz walnuts, chopped roughly	boiling
25 g/1 oz butter	250 g/8 oz pumpkin or other
1 onion, chopped	squash flesh, de-seeded and
1 tbsp chopped fresh sage	chopped roughly
400 g/14 oz arborio (risotto) rice	75 g/3 oz Stilton cheese, crumbled
	4 sprigs of fresh sage, to garnish

❶ Heat the oil in a large pan and brown the walnuts – about 5 minutes. Set aside on a plate.

❷ Add the butter, onion and chopped sage to the pan and soften for 6–8 minutes. Stir in the rice to absorb the cooking juices, then the stock and pumpkin. Simmer for 15 minutes, uncovered, stirring frequently.

❸ Remove from the heat, stir in the crumbled Stilton and half the walnuts and leave covered for 5 minutes to warm through. Garnish with sage sprigs and the remaining walnuts and enjoy with a glass of Italian red wine.

CARAMELISED MUSHROOM TATINS

This is a recipe for the keen cook, as it involves several kitchen procedures (though nothing fiendish) and it was discovered and developed by none other than my mother. As regular readers may know, the mother in question is my official tester, responsible for double testing every Daily Express *recipe, so it comes as no surprise that she is a skilled inventor of recipes in her own right, when occasionally she finds time to set herself loose.*

FOR THE KEEN COOK: *allow 1¹/₂ hours*

SERVES 4

1 large and 1 small onion	¹/₂ tsp dried thyme
3 tbsp olive oil	250 g/8 oz mushrooms, sliced
75 ml/2¹/₂ fl oz chicken stock	a sheet of ready-rolled puff pastry
1 tsp wine vinegar, plus a	4 tbsp sugar
little extra	salt and pepper
1 garlic clove, chopped	

❶ Slice the large onion thinly. Heat 1 tbsp of the oil in a pan and fry the onion till very soft – 10 minutes. Add the chicken stock and 1 tsp of the vinegar, season well and cook gently until the liquid has evaporated and onion is very tender. Set aside.

❷ Chop the small onion finely. Heat the remaining oil in the same pan, fry the onion for 5 minutes, add the garlic and thyme and cook for 2 minutes. Add the mushrooms and cook gently for 10 minutes. Preheat the oven to 220°C/200°fan oven/Gas Mark 7.

❸ Get out four 125 ml/4 fl oz capacity ramekins and use one to cut out four circles from the puff pastry.

❹ Combine the sugar and 1 tbsp of water in a small saucepan over a medium heat. Swirl until the sugar has completely dissolved, then boil until it caramelises and turns nut brown: go easy as you approach this and keep taking the pan off the heat as, if you miss your moment, it will go too dark and you'll have to start step 4 again (see Tip). Swirl ¼ tsp vinegar into the caramel and allow to cool for 1 minute – then pour into the base of the ramekins. Top with the onion and then the mushroom mixtures.

5 Lay pastry circles over the mushroom mixture and bake on a baking sheet for 25–30 minutes, till puffed and golden. Cool for a minute and then invert and unmould on to serving plates; serve warm or at room temperature.

T I P When making caramel, it is a good idea to have a large heatproof bowl of cold water to hand. The moment the caramel achieves the desired colour, plunge the bottom of the pan in the water to arrest cooking – watch out for steam and hissing!

WINTER VEGETABLE CURRY

Our ancestors in prehistoric times used autumn to store up energy for the bleak months until spring arrived, and I think we retain that urge for satisfying, filling hot meals to this day. This recipe is, however, low in fat.

EASY: *allow 45 minutes; freezes well*

SERVES 6

2 tbsp oil

1 onion, chopped

1 garlic clove, chopped

2.5 cm/1-inch piece of root ginger, chopped

1 tsp cumin seeds

1 tsp mustard seeds (from Indian shops)

2 tbsp curry paste

200 g can of chopped tomatoes

3 carrots, peeled

3 parsnips, peeled

½ green cabbage

salt and pepper

chopped fresh coriander, to serve

❶ Heat the oil, add the onion and fry gently for 10 minutes, till lightly browned – don't turn up the heat or it will scorch. Stir in the garlic, ginger, cumin and mustard seeds and fry for a few minutes more. Stir in the curry paste and tomatoes, then add 300 ml/½ pint of water and seasoning. Bring to the boil, then simmer for 10 minutes.

❷ Cut the carrots and parsnips into chunks. Separate the cabbage leaves and cut in pieces. Boil the carrots and parsnips in salted water for 10 minutes, add the cabbage and cook for 3–5 minutes. Drain and tip into a serving dish. Pour over the curry sauce and top with the coriander. Serve with basmati rice.

TIP To flavour the rice, either add a pinch of saffron to the water, or add a cinnamon stick and ½ tsp of cardamom seeds, a clove and bay leaf. Serve with the spices still in the rice – but don't eat them.

chapter 5

SPECIAL SUNDAY LUNCHES

Sunday lunch has made a comeback. It is a time for scattered families to gather, and for friends to share relaxed time together. For the cook, it is the best meal of the week; you've the whole morning to prepare for it, and the whole afternoon (and evening if you like!) to enjoy eating it.

Roasts remain a favourite, and the newer cuts mean faster cooking times and less waste. But there are other approaches to Sunday lunch too – slow-cooking stews and smaller cuts of meat. Sunday lunch also requires a dessert, and you'll find suggestions in the Dashing Desserts chapter (pages 137–154).

BEEF BRAISED IN
GUINNESS, WITH PRUNES

*This is a wonderful traditional beef casserole in which the tang of
Guinness is complemented by the sweet richness of prunes. Like all
stews, it can be made in advance, cooled and chilled, then reheated.
Quite simply, this is my favourite stew in the world, and it was
invented by my friend (and one of the best cooks in all the world)
Mary Cadogan.*

EASY: *allow 25 minutes to prepare, 2–2¹/₂ hours to cook; freezes well*

SERVES 6

1.05 kg/2¼ lb braising steak	1 tbsp tomato purée
1 tbsp plain flour, seasoned	2 tsp ready-made mustard
2 tbsp oil	a bouquet garni
25 g/1 oz butter	2 tsp brown sugar
2 onions, sliced	125 g/4 oz pitted ready-to-eat prunes
2 carrots, diced	salt and pepper
300 ml/½ pint Guinness	handful of fresh parsley, chopped,
425 ml/¾ pint stock	to garnish

❶ Cut the steak into large chunks about 5 cm/2 inches across and toss in
the seasoned flour. Heat the oil and butter in a large flameproof casserole,
add the onions and cook for 5 minutes until browned. Add the meat and
cook till brown all over.

❷ Add the carrots, then gradually stir in the beer, stock, purée, mustard,
bouquet garni, sugar, salt and pepper. Bring to the boil, stir well and cover
tightly with a lid. Simmer gently for 1½ hours, stirring occasionally.

❸ Add the prunes and simmer for a further ½–1 hour, until the meat is
tender. Serve sprinkled with parsley.

TIP 🥣 Mixing oil and butter as a medium for frying gives the
advantages of both. Butter contributes flavour, the oil allows you to
cook at a higher heat without burning.

CHEDDAR CHEESE AND VEGETABLE ROAST

This recipe is a hearty vegetarian bake based on Cheddar, which remains in my opinion the cheese for cooking par excellence. I am indebted for the recipe to Fiona McCowan of Gloucestershire.

VERY EASY: *allow 1 hour*

SERVES 4

3 tbsp oil	250 g/8 oz fresh breadcrumbs (Fiona
1 green pepper, chopped finely	uses granary or wholemeal)
1 red pepper, chopped finely	175 g/6 oz mature Cheddar cheese,
1 onion, chopped finely	grated
375 g/12 oz mushrooms, chopped	1 large egg
3 celery sticks, chopped small	salt and pepper

1 Preheat the oven to 190°C/170°C fan oven/Gas Mark 5. Heat the oil in a large frying pan and cook the peppers and onion in the hot oil for 5 minutes.

2 Add the mushrooms and celery and fry until the vegetables are tender, keeping the heat low. Allow about 10 minutes.

3 Remove from the heat and add three-quarters of the breadcrumbs and two-thirds of the cheese. Beat the egg with salt and pepper and mix in well.

4 Spoon the mixture into a 1.25-litre/2-pint ovenproof dish. Mix together the remaining breadcrumbs and cheese and sprinkle on top.

5 Bake for 25 minutes until golden brown.

TIP 🥄 Making breadcrumbs is a messy business. I tend to get out the processor or blender and whizz a lot at once, and freeze what I don't need in a freezer bag. These can be used from frozen when you just need a small quantity.

CRISP ROAST DUCK

This recipe is based on a southern French idea and, although it is unconventional in several respects, I hope you will trust me and give it a go. Although the cooking time seems eternal, the preparations are minimal, and I know no other way of making one duck feed four comfortably. Incidentally, if you love crispy duck, this is the way to make it, regardless of the sauce.

DIFFERENT AND DELICIOUS: *(for the duck)10 minutes to prepare, 4 hours in the oven; meanwhile (for the sauce) 20 minutes to prepare, 2 hours simmering*

SERVES 4

1 large duck	2 tbsp plain flour
salt	900 ml/1½ pints chicken stock
For the braised olive sauce:	a bottle of white wine
2 tbsp oil	2 bay leaves
1 kg/2 lb chicken wings or	a bouquet garni
drumsticks	salt, pepper and lemon juice
2 large onions, sliced	200 g can of green olives, drained

❶ Start the duck 4 hours before lunch or dinner. Heat the oven to 120°C/100°C fan oven/if cooking by gas, set the switch between Gas Mark ¼ and ½. This seems very low but it works. Trim any fat from inside the duck – butchers often stick a few bits there and it is not required for this recipe. Rub all over with salt, including inside the duck. Prick all over lightly so you prick the skin but don't penetrate the meat (easiest if you keep the skewer almost flat to the skin, rather than sticking in at 90 degrees). Roast, breast-side down, on a rack, for 3 hours, pricking lightly occasionally. Turn the oven up to 180°C/160°C fan oven/Gas Mark 4, turn duck breast-side up and roast for 45 minutes to crisp the duck. Rest for 10 minutes before carving.

❷ Start the sauce once the duck is in the oven. Fry the chicken in the oil for 10–15 minutes, till a rich brown. Remove from the pan and cook the onions in the remaining oil. Stir in the flour, then return the chicken to the pan and add the stock, wine and herbs. Simmer uncovered for 2 hours, then strain. Spoon off any fat and season well (see step 3), adding lemon juice to sharpen if you wish.

❸ The olives can be left whole or chopped and added just to warm through. The French tend to boil them for a couple of minutes to get rid of excess salt, but I do not find this necessary, as long as you take account of this when seasoning the sauce.

❹ Carve the duck – the skin is as delectable as the flesh – and serve with the sauce. I find rice the ideal accompaniment, rather than roast potatoes.

T I P 🥣 I wish butchers wouldn't slip unwanted bits of fat into the cavity of a chicken or duck before selling, presumably to make up the weight. It serves no purpose and is a bit like that practice of putting the leanest pieces of meat at the top of a packet of stewing steak. Yet another reason – as if we needed one – to patronise our local butcher on every possible occasion.

HERB - CRUSTED LAMB

For this rather elegant variation on roast lamb, you need to find loin fillets. I am indebted for the idea to a favourite cook of mine, Amy Willcock of the George Hotel at Yarmouth in the Isle of Wight.

NOT DIFFICULT: *allow 40 minutes*

SERVES 6

6 lamb loin fillets

1 garlic clove, peeled

1 onion, cut in quarters

2 rashers of smoked streaky bacon, cut up roughly

1 tbsp each chopped fresh basil and mint

1 slice of white bread, roughly broken up

2 tbsp grated parmesan cheese

2 tbsp softened butter

salt and pepper

1 If not preparing ahead, preheat the oven to 220°C/200°C fan oven/ Gas Mark 7. Trim the fillets of fat and any sinews.

2 The crust is made in the processor. Whizz the garlic first till scattered in the bowl, then put in all remaining ingredients plus seasoning and process till chopped roughly together. Press on top of each fillet and put on a baking sheet. You can prepare ahead up to this point and refrigerate, if convenient.

3 Put the fillets in the hot oven for 12–15 minutes. Serve on a bed of mashed potatoes with a fresh vegetable of your choice.

TIP For this dish or a more traditional roast lamb you might like to try Amy's Chunky Mint Sauce: fry a chopped onion in 50 g/2 oz of butter till very soft but not coloured (keep heat low – 10 minutes). Add 2 tbsp of chopped fresh mint, 1 tsp of caster sugar and seasoning. Whizz till smooth and serve warm.

MAHOGANY ROAST CHICKEN

Here is a really different, one might say revolutionary, take on roast chicken. At first it may sound a bit of a palaver: you need to start a day ahead, and you need a very large pot capable of taking a whole chicken covered with water. Given that, you simply soak the chicken overnight in a flavoured mixture, remove, drain and roast. Result: a beautifully flavoured, meltingly tender bird, and no one would ever guess how you achieved it.

START THE DAY BEFORE: *10 minutes to prepare, about 1 hour 10 minutes to cook*

DEPENDING ON SIZE OF CHICKEN,
SERVES 4 – 5

1 roasting chicken
butter, melted
salt and pepper
For the brine:
about 4 litres/8 pints water
75 g/3 oz salt

125 g/4 oz granulated sugar
125 g/4 oz black treacle
2 tbsp soy sauce (I find Kikkoman's
the best)
1 tbsp Tabasco sauce

❶ Mix the water, salt, sugar, treacle, soy sauce and Tabasco and add the chicken. Refrigerate for 12–24 hours.

❷ Remove the chicken from the brine and discard the liquid. Dry well inside and out. Preheat the oven to 190ºC/170ºC fan oven/Gas Mark 5. Preheat a roasting pan. Brush chicken all over with melted butter, season and put upside-down on a rack, resting on one breast. Put into the roasting tin and roast for 20 minutes on one breast.

❸ Roll the chicken over to its other breast and cook for another 20 minutes. Finish cooking for 20–30 minutes the correct way up until cooked. Do not baste the bird.

❹ Serve with gravy made in the usual way.

PORK WITH OLIVES

This a really tasty, slow-cooked casserole for a winter evening.

EASY AND COMFORTING: *20 minutes to prepare, 1¹/₂ hours to cook; freezes well*

SERVES 4

2 tbsp oil

4 large pork chops, meat cut off the bone, trimmed and cut in large cubes, or 500 g/1 lb pork shoulder

1 onion, sliced thinly

1 garlic clove, chopped

1 tsp brown sugar

2 tbsp flour

400 g can of tomatoes

a glass of red wine

2 bay leaves

1 cinnamon stick

125 g/4 oz stuffed olives or your favourites, drained, rinsed and dried

salt and pepper

❶ Preheat the oven to 140°C/120°C fan oven/Gas Mark 1. Heat half the oil in a large pan and brown the cubes of pork till a lovely toasty brown on all sides – about 5 minutes. Remove to a casserole. In same pan, heat the remaining oil and, over a lower heat, lightly brown the onion, garlic and sugar – about 6–7 minutes.

❷ Stir in the flour, mix well and heat for 2–3 minutes till beginning to toast. Stir in the tomatoes and their juice, breaking down the tomatoes well with a wooden spoon, till the mixture begins to thicken and comes to the boil. Add the wine and bring to the boil, then pour over the pork. Add the bay leaves and cinnamon, cover and cook in the oven for 1¹/₂ hours. Uncover, stir in the olives and put in the oven for a further half hour.

❸ Check the seasoning. Pork varies and it may be that the stew is too liquid or too stiff. The latter is easily corrected by stirring in a little extra red wine. If too thin, put a colander over a wide saucepan and ladle in the stew. Boil the sauce hard to reduce to the desired consistency – this won't take more than 5 minutes. Remove bay leaves and cinnamon stick and serve with rice, baked potatoes or mash.

ROAST PORK FILLET, WITH PARSNIP MASH

Here is an alternative idea for lunch this Sunday: a lovely autumn combination of British pork and apples.

FUN TO MAKE: *allow 45 minutes*

SERVES 4

2 British pork fillets (about
  750 g/ 1½ lb), trimmed of
  fat and sinews
½ tsp ground allspice
a little oil
salt and pepper
For the parsnip mash:
750 g/1½ lb) parsnips, peeled
  and chopped
400 g/14 oz potatoes, peeled
  and chopped

142 ml carton of single cream
25 g/1 oz butter
¼ tsp ground nutmeg
salt
For the apples:
40 g/1½ oz butter
2 Cox's Orange Pippins, cored
  and cut in wedges
1 tbsp brown sugar
2 tbsp white wine

❶ Preheat the oven to 180°C/160°C fan oven/Gas Mark 4. For the mash, cook the parsnips and potatoes together in boiling, salted water till soft, then drain and mash. Stir in cream, butter and nutmeg and warm through.

❷ Sprinkle the pork fillets with allspice and seasoning. Heat the oil in a pan and brown the fillets all over for about 3–4 minutes – then transfer to a roasting pan and roast for just 10 minutes, till tender. Set aside for 10 minutes before serving.

❸ For the apples, heat the butter in a frying pan – the one in which you fried the pork is fine – add the apples, sprinkle with sugar and cook over high heat for 5–10 minutes, till well browned and the sauce is starting to caramelise. Stir in the wine and simmer for a minute.

❹ To serve, put the mash on four plates, top with the pork, cut in slices, and apples, and drizzle over the sauce.

SOY ROASTED FILLET OF BEEF

Fillet of beef is the most luxurious cut of all – and the rule is to keep everything around it really simple. Here, herbs and soy add all the flavouring you could wish for.

SIMPLE BUT LUXURIOUS: *allow time to marinate, then roast for 15–20 minutes according to taste*

SERVES 3 – 4

For the marinade:

50 ml/2 fl oz Kikkoman soy sauce

2 tbsp olive oil

chopped fresh thyme, parsley, chives

For the beef:

550 g/1 lb 2oz fillet of beef

1 tbsp olive oil

1 Mix the marinade ingredients and add the beef. Marinate for at least an hour, or overnight if more convenient – you can do this in a shallow bowl covered with plastic film or in a strong plastic bag.

2 When ready to cook, remove the beef, pat dry on kitchen paper and discard the marinade, which will have done its job. Preheat the oven to 200°C/180°C fan oven/Gas Mark Mark 6. In a small frying pan, heat the oil to very hot (be warned, it does spit quite a bit) and brown the beef all over – about 4 minutes in total.

3 Transfer to the oven and cook for 15–20 minutes, till done to your liking. Carve in slices to serve. The ideal accompaniment is mashed potato.

T I P Fillet of beef is best ordered from the butcher in advance. If you have a choice, specify Aberdeen Angus or organic.

STUFFED PORK TENDERLOIN

Here is a more adventurous idea for pork tenderloin, in which you make a hole down the centre of the tenderloin and stuff as you wish. This makes an excellent easy idea for a dinner party, as it can be prepared in advance, chilled if necessary, brought back to room temperature and then simply roasted at step 3.

FUN AND DELICIOUS: *20 minutes to prepare, 40 minutes to cook*

SERVES 4

1 large pork tenderloin, about
   550 g/1 lb 2 oz
1 small red pepper, de-seeded and
   diced finely
7 olives, pitted and chopped

1 large garlic clove, crushed
1 tbsp pine kernels, toasted
1 tbsp chopped fresh parsley
50 g/2 oz feta cheese, crumbled
salt and pepper

1 Trim excess fat and gristle from the tenderloin. Mix the stuffing ingredients in a small bowl and season well. Put into a strong plastic bag, seal or tie the end and snip a hole in one corner – you will be using this as a piping bag. Refrigerate till ready to use.

2 Preheat the oven to 220°C/200°C fan oven/Gas Mark 7. Insert a long thin knife into the centre of the loin to make a hole, then widen with a wooden spoon handle. Pipe in the stuffing, then tie the pork, not too tightly, in several places and round the length as well.

3 Roast for about 40 minutes; leave to rest for 5–10 minutes before slicing fairly thinly and serving.

TIP 🥄 If you can only find smaller tenderloins, use two and reduce the cooking time to 30–35 minutes.

STUFFED LEG OF LAMB

This recipe has a pleasant Biblical feel to it, incorporating subtle Middle-Eastern flavours and juicy fresh dates. This is very much a special-occasion roast; because the leg is boned it is far easier to carve. SPECIAL AND DELICIOUS: *25 minutes to prepare, 1 hour 20 minutes to roast, plus resting time.*

SERVES 6 – 8

1.75 kg/4 lb leg of lamb, boned
  (see Tip)
1 tbsp good olive oil
salt and pepper
For the spinach stuffing:
250 g/8 oz fresh spinach, or frozen
1 tbsp good olive oil
1 small onion, chopped
1 small celery stick, chopped
  (optional)

2 garlic cloves, crushed
50 g/2 oz pistachio nuts, chopped
50 g/2 oz fresh white breadcrumbs
  (2 thick slices of bread, crusts off)
½ tsp dried mint
½ tsp ground cinnamon
125 g/4 oz fresh dates, stoned
  and chopped
salt and pepper

❶ Remove the lamb from the refrigerator and season all over.

❷ The stuffing can be made in advance. Wash the spinach, if using fresh, and cook until soft – this can be as quick as 3 minutes. Drain in a colander and push down well to dry. If using frozen, either defrost and drain, or cook from frozen and drain.

❸ Fry the onion, celery (if you have any lying round – not worth buying specially) and garlic over a gentle heat for 5 minutes until tender but not browned. Add the nuts, breadcrumbs, mint, cinnamon and seasoning and cook for 3 minutes longer, till beginning to smell aromatic. Stir in the spinach and dates and your stuffing is ready. If not proceeding at once, cool and refrigerate.

❹ Preheat the oven to 190°C/170°C fan oven/Gas Mark 5. Use your hands to stuff the lamb – you will have a little more stuffing than you need, but pack it in as best you can regardless, as stuffing always proves popular. Tie up the lamb to a squarish shape, keeping the stuffing in as much as possible.

❺ Heat the oil in a frying pan and brown the lamb on top and bottom; transfer to a rack in a roasting tin. Roast for 1 hour 10 minutes, basting three times. Use a small sharp knife to check the lamb is cooked to your satisfaction and set aside for 20 minutes before carving, which also gives you time to make gravy. Carve straight down the lamb in medium slices to serve.

T I P S ⬭ If you have any choice in the boning of the leg, ask your butcher to cut out the bone leaving a hole (so the leg looks like a giant Polo mint) rather than making it into a large flat piece. Alternatively, make up the stuffing in advance and ask him to roll it for you: get him to pack in as much as he can and not to tie it too tightly, as butchers tend to pride themselves on prize fighter knots.

The most amazing fresh dates appear in the shops nowadays; best for this recipe are Medjool dates, from Tunisia among other countries. Alternatively, use the dates that come in those long elliptical boxes with a peculiar plastic fork included.

LAMB GOULASH

Instead of a roast, it can be nice to serve a stew for Sunday lunch.
This is simple but reassuring with plenty of good boiled potatoes or
your favourite accompaniment.
EASY: *allow 1¹/₂ hours; freezes well*

SERVES 4

1 kg/2 lb lamb neck fillet	150 ml/¼ pint red wine or stock
2 tbsp oil	400 g can of whole tomatoes
2 onions	142 ml carton of plain yogurt
1 dessertspoon flour	(not low-fat)
2 dessertspoons paprika	chopped fresh parsley, to garnish

❶ Cut the lamb into cubes, removing any fat and gristle. Heat the oil in
a frying pan and brown the lamb in it gently, till browned on all sides.
Remove with a slotted spoon and put into a lidded casserole. Preheat
the oven to 160°C/150°C fan oven/Gas Mark 3.

❷ Slice the onions and put into the frying pan; cook for 5 minutes, then
blend in the flour and the paprika. Gradually add the wine or stock, stirring
to make a smooth sauce. Season to taste and pour over the lamb.

❸ Drain the tomatoes and add to the casserole, then cover and cook for
about an hour, till the lamb is tender. Stir in the yogurt to heat through,
then serve the goulash sprinkled with chopped parsley, with noodles,
rice or potatoes.

> **TIP** 🥣 When I visited Budapest I ate 'real' goulash and was
> surprised to find that it is a soup rather than a stew. But the keynote
> flavourings of paprika, lamb and tomatoes are what gives it its
> essential Hungarian character.

chapter 6

IMPRESSIVE LUNCH AND DINNER PARTIES

A few years ago 'impressive' was a taboo word in the cook's dictionary, conjuring up visions of decorated savoury mousses or Van Dyck lemons (the ones halved in zigzags like Jacobean ruffs).

I think it is fine for the cook to wish to impress, but through skill and flavour rather than time-consuming garnishes. All the dishes in this chapter require a little planning; many can be completed before the meal, others are finished off before your guests' eyes, because there are occasions for both.

They are a little bit more work than some of the others but I never believe in putting anyone through a cooking process unless it is necessary, so I hope you will enjoy the making as much as your guests the eating.

MINCED LAMB PASTA BAKE

*I have never found a bought cheese sauce I am happy with (unlike
tomato sauces, which I find increasingly acceptable) but, if you have
a favourite, you can spare yourself the trouble of making the sauce in
step 3; you will need about 300 ml/¹/₂ pint.*

EASY AND THRIFTY: *ready in under an hour*

SERVES 4

550 g/1 lb 2oz lamb mince, fresh or frozen	**salt and freshly ground black pepper**
	For the cheese sauce:
300 ml/¹/₂ pint carton of spicy tomato (Arabbiata-type) sauce	**1 tbsp flour**
	1 tbsp butter
1 tbsp tomato purée	**300 ml/¹/₂ pint milk**
375 g/12 oz dried penne pasta	**50 g/2 oz Cheddar cheese, grated**
6 tbsp ready-grated parmesan cheese	**a good pinch of ground nutmeg**

❶ Preheat the oven to 200°C/180°C fan oven/Gas Mark 6. Fry the
mince without added oil for 10 minutes over a medium heat, until
thawed (if frozen) and browned. Drain any oil from the pan, add the
tomato sauce and purée and simmer for 10 minutes to reduce, stirring
occasionally. Season.

❷ Meanwhile, cook the pasta according to packet directions (even the
same shape of pasta takes a different time to cook depending on make)
and drain.

❸ Make the cheese sauce by whisking together the flour, butter and
milk over a lowish heat – don't stop till it is smooth and thick. Stir in
the Cheddar and nutmeg.

❹ To assemble, take a large ovenproof dish. Put in half the pasta, sprinkle
with a third of the parmesan and season with black pepper. Spoon half
the meat mixture over the top. Repeat. Now spoon the cheese sauce
over the whole thing and sprinkle with remaining parmesan. Bake for
15 minutes, till golden and bubbling.

CHICKEN CACCIATORE

'Hunter's chicken': a full-blooded chicken casserole flavoured with mushrooms and enriched with tomatoes and red wine. This is just the thing for a dismal autumn evening. Chicken thighs are economical and tastier than chicken breasts.

NOT DIFFICULT: *allow 1¹/4 hours; freezes well*

SERVES 4 – 6

8 chicken thighs (not boneless), trimmed of excess fat

1 tbsp olive oil

1 onion, chopped

3 large field mushrooms, cut in 2 cm/³/4-inch cubes

4 garlic cloves, chopped finely

1¹/2 tbsp plain flour

250 ml/8 fl oz red wine

125 ml/4 fl oz chicken stock

400 g can of tomatoes, drained

a piece of parmesan cheese rind (see Tip)

2 tsp chopped fresh sage

salt and pepper

❶ Season the chicken well. Heat the oil in a casserole over a medium heat then add half the chicken thighs and cook, not moving them, until the underside is crisp and brown – about 5 minutes. Flip over for another 5 minutes. Set aside and repeat with the remaining thighs.

❷ Drain all but 1 tbsp of oil from the casserole. Add the onion, mushrooms and a sprinkling of salt. Fry for 6–8 minutes, till beginning to brown. Add the garlic and cook for just 30 seconds, then the flour, for 1 minute. Add the wine, scraping bottom of pan to loosen any burnt bits, then the stock, tomatoes, thyme, parmesan rind (if using) and pepper.

❸ Add the chicken pieces and spoon the sauce over them. Cover, turn the heat to low and simmer for 45 minutes, till the chicken is cooked through, turning the chicken pieces at half time. Fish out the cheese rind, stir in the sage, check the seasoning and serve.

> **T I P** 🥄 A brilliant destiny for the hard bit of parmesan rind that can't be grated. Just remember to throw it away at the end.

CHICKEN BRAISED IN LAGER

If you like that nice, malty beer taste, make this as a dark and delectable change from coq au vin.

NOT DIFFICULT: *15 minutes to prepare, 1 hour to cook*

SERVES 4

1.25 kg/3 lb free-range chicken, quartered

50 g/2 oz butter

a little oil

4 shallots, chopped finely

2 garlic cloves, crushed

275 g/9 oz mushrooms, sliced

440 ml can of lager or pale ale

75 ml/2½ fl oz gin

142 ml carton of single cream

½ tsp sugar

salt and pepper

chopped fresh parsley, to garnish

❶ Brown the chicken pieces in a deep casserole in the butter and oil for 5 minutes per side – don't move until it is time to turn them over. Remove from the pan and add the shallots, garlic and mushrooms: cook for a good 5 minutes. Return the chicken to the pan and add all but 2 tbsp of the lager and the gin. Season and simmer, covered, for an hour (either on the hob or in an oven preheated to 160°C/140°C fan oven/Gas Mark 3), until the chicken is tender.

❷ Remove the chicken and mushrooms to a serving dish and keep hot. Degrease the juices, either by skimming or straining into a jug and removing the juices with a bulb baster, discarding the fat that will rise to the surface. Boil the juices fast till reduced by half (you will probably start with about 300 ml/½ pint) and then whisk in the cream and remaining lager. Check the seasoning, add the sugar and pour over the chicken; then sprinkle with parsley and serve with pasta or rice to absorb the delicious juices.

CHICKEN MARSALA

This dish is quite simply a dinner-party classic: simple but wonderful flavours in complete harmony.

WORTH THE TROUBLE: *allow 45 minutes*

SERVES 4, IN STYLE

50 g/2 oz plain flour	1 tsp tomato purée
4 boneless, skinless chicken breasts	350 ml/12 fl oz marsala
(about 150 g/5 oz each)	1½ tbsp lemon juice
2 tbsp vegetable oil	50 g/2 oz butter, at room
3 slices of pancetta or streaky	temperature
smoked bacon, cut in strips	2 tbsp chopped fresh parsley
250 g/8 oz mushrooms, sliced	salt and pepper
1 garlic clove, crushed	

❶ Put a large heatproof plate into the oven and heat the oven to 100°C/80°C fan oven/Gas Mark ¼. Heat a large frying pan until very hot. Dry the chicken breasts on kitchen paper, season well and dip in the flour all over. Shake to remove excess flour. Add the oil to the hot pan and let it get hot, then add the chicken and cook for 3 minutes. Flip over for 3 minutes longer. Transfer to the heated plate and pop in the oven to keep warm

❷ Return the pan to a low heat and fry the pancetta for about 4–5 minutes. Transfer to a plate lined with kitchen paper. Add the mushrooms, increase the heat to hot and fry hard for 8 minutes. During this time the mushrooms will release water, and then boil dry and start to brown: this is correct. Add the garlic, tomato purée and cooked pancetta. Cook for a minute and then, off the heat, add the marsala and scrape all the solids from the side of the pan to deglaze. Boil till reduced to about 300 ml/½ pint. Off the heat, add the lemon juice and any juices on the chicken plate, then whisk in butter, 1 tbsp at a time. Season, stir in the parsley, pour over the chicken and serve.

CHICKEN PAILLARD

This simple chicken dish requires just five ingredients, including a simple tomato and goat's cheese salad to accompany it. It takes about 40 minutes to put together and if you don't mind disappearing for a few minutes before you eat, this is an elegant dish for entertaining. In this case, serve on a bed of lettuce leaves.

NOT DIFFICULT: *allow 40 minutes*

SERVES 4

4 skinless, boneless chicken breasts

250 g/8 oz cherry tomatoes, halved

250 g/8 oz small plum tomatoes, halved

50 g/2 oz mild goat's cheese, crumbled

3 tbsp extra-virgin olive oil

salt and pepper

❶ Beat out each chicken breast between sheets of cling film to about 1 cm/½ inch thick, using a rolling pin.

❷ Put the tomatoes in a colander over a bowl, sprinkle with salt and leave to drain. Whisk half the goat's cheese into the tomato juices until smooth, followed by 2 tbsp of the oil. Season. Fold the tomatoes and remaining goat's cheese into the mixture.

❸ Heat the grill, brush the chicken with the remaining oil and season. Grill for about 5 minutes, turning once, until done to your liking. Serve accompanied by the goat's cheese dressing and potatoes.

> **T I P** 🥄 *Paillard* refers to the beating out of the chicken breasts into escalopes – a brilliant way to tenderise the meat and speed up cooking.

COD AND TOMATO STEW

This is an easy and reliable dish for an informal supper party.

EASY: *30 minutes from start to finish*

SERVES 4

2 tbsp olive oil

2 onions, chopped

400 g can of chopped tomatoes

1 tbsp soy sauce

1 tsp fresh thyme leaves, chopped,
  or ½ tsp dried thyme

4 skinless cod fillets, about 175 g/
  6 oz each

salt and pepper

❶ Heat the olive oil in a wide pan and fry the onions for 10 minutes, stirring occasionally, until softened and lightly browned. Stir in the tomatoes, soy sauce, thyme, salt and pepper.

❷ Bring to the boil and simmer, uncovered, for 5 minutes until slightly thickened.

❸ Slide the cod fillets into the pan, cover with a lid or foil and cook gently for about 5 minutes, until the cod is tender and flakes easily. Serve with potatoes or noodles.

TIP 🥣 The quality of canned tomatoes varies widely – avoid the cheaper types.

BEEF CURRY FROM KERALA

This is a special-occasion curry from India's south. It is not wet and soupy, but dry and aromatic, and excellent accompanied by basmati rice and yogurt mixed with diced cucumber.

NOT DIFFICULT: *allow 1¹/₂ hours; make a day ahead and reheat if convenient, or freezes well*

SERVES 4 – 6

625 g/1¹/₂ lb boneless beef (such as top rump), cut in 2 cm/³/₄-inch cubes

4 tsp ground coriander

¹/₂ tsp ground cumin

¹/₂ tsp cayenne pepper

¹/₂ tsp fennel seeds, ground with a pestle and mortar

¹/₄ tsp turmeric

1¹/₄ tsp salt

2 tbsp oil

25 g/1 oz butter

¹/₂ cinnamon stick

3 cloves

2 onions, sliced thinly

2 cm/³/₄ inch cube of fresh ginger, peeled and chopped

2 garlic cloves, chopped

2 fresh hot green chillies, split lengthways and de-seeded

juice of ¹/₂ lime

salt and pepper

1 Put the first seven ingredients in a large pot with 250 ml/8 fl oz of water and bring to the boil. Simmer, covered, for 15 minutes; then set aside uncovered.

2 Heat the oil and butter in a large frying pan. Add the cinnamon and cloves and fry till fragrant – about 2 minutes – then add the onions and fry till lightly browned – about 7 minutes. Reduce the heat and add the ginger, garlic and chillies and cook for 20 minutes longer, stirring frequently, until the onions are well browned.

3 Set aside 50 ml/2 fl oz of the beef cooking liquid, then add the meat and its juices to the frying pan. Cook for about 20–30 minutes, stirring frequently, until the liquid reduces to a thick sauce and the meat is tender. Add a little of the reserved cooking liquid if the meat gets too dry before it becomes tender. Check the seasoning and add lime juice to serve.

LAMB AND RED
PEPPER STEW

There is a lot to be said for an all-in-one stew, in which you combine warming flavours and let them meld and merge on the hob.

EASY: *allow 50 minutes, including 30 minutes cooking; can be made ahead, frozen and reheated*

SERVES 4

875 g/1¾ lb boneless lamb fillet, cut in small chunks

25 g/1 oz plain flour, seasoned

3 tbsp olive oil

3 garlic cloves, crushed

150 ml/¼ pint dry white wine

3 small red peppers, de-seeded and cut in 5 cm/2-inch pieces

150 ml/¼ pint passata

250 ml/8 fl oz stock (lamb, chicken or vegetable)

3 bay leaves

125 g/4 oz ready-to-eat prunes or apricots

salt and pepper

❶ Put the cubes of lamb into a plastic bag with the seasoned flour and shake vigorously until the lamb is evenly coated.

❷ Heat the oil in large saucepan or flameproof casserole dish. Add half the lamb and fry, turning now and then, until nicely browned all over. Lift on to a plate and repeat with the remaining lamb. Return the first batch of meat to the pan with the garlic and cook for 1 minute. Add any flour left in the bag and cook for another minute.

❸ Pour the wine into the pan and cook over a high heat until it has reduced by about one third. Stir in the red peppers, passata, stock, bay leaves and a little seasoning. Cover and simmer for 30 minutes or until the lamb is tender. Add the prunes or apricots and simmer for a further 5 minutes. Serve with rice, mash or jacket potatoes.

> **T I P** 🥄 As a variation, use chicken instead of lamb and reduce the cooking time to 20 minutes.

OLD-FASHIONED
CHICKEN PIE

This sumptuous recipe is for the enthusiastic cook, as it involves several stages of preparation. Everything about it is the best, so save for a really special occasion.

ELABORATE BUT WORTH THE TROUBLE: *make pastry in advance, 1 hour to prepare, 30 minutes to cook; freezes well*

SERVES 6

For the flaky pastry (see Tip):

175 g/6 oz butter

250 g/8 oz plain flour

½ tsp salt

For the filling:

2 sausages

1 slice of bread, crusts off, made into crumbs

a good pinch of mixed dried herbs

1 egg yolk

25 g/1 oz butter

2 skinless, boneless chicken breasts

3 hard-boiled eggs, quartered

125 g/4 oz cooked tongue – not sliced, but cut in cubes (optional)

For the sauce:

40 g/1½ oz butter

2 tbsp plain flour

350 ml/12 fl oz chicken stock

juice of ½ lemon

chopped fresh parsley

salt and pepper

1 egg, beaten, to glaze

❶ Make the pastry. Wrap the butter in foil and put in the freezer for 45 minutes. Put the flour in a deep wide bowl and mix in the salt. Holding the frozen butter in the foil, dip it in the flour and grate coarsely over the flour. Continue to dip in the flour and grate, peeling back the foil as necessary so it doesn't get grated in. When you have finished, lightly mix all together so the butter is evenly coated in flour, then stir in 8–9 tbsp cold water to form a dough. Gently form into a ball without kneading, wrap in plastic film and chill for 30 minutes.

❷ Make the filling. Remove skins from sausages and mix with the breadcrumbs, herbs and yolk to form a paste. Roll into 12 small balls with wetted hands. Heat the butter in a large frying pan and fry the chicken till golden – 5 minutes – then add the balls. Turning everything often, cook for 10 minutes, by which time the balls should be brown and the chicken cooked. Remove the chicken and balls from the pan, reserving the juices, and leave to cool. Slice the chicken on the diagonal.

3 Make the sauce by putting the butter, flour and stock in the frying pan (so as not to waste the delicious juices from the chicken) and whisking constantly till it thickens. Simmer for 10 minutes to thicken a little more and add lemon juice and parsley. Season to taste.

4 Preheat the oven to 200°C/180°C fan oven/Gas Mark 6. Arrange the chicken, sausage balls, quartered eggs and tongue, if using, in a large dish; pour over the sauce.

5 Roll out the pastry on a lightly floured board. Brush the rim of the dish with egg, lay a narrow pastry strip all the way around the rim, brush again with egg and lay the pastry over the top. Decorate if you wish, glaze with more egg, cut a slit in the centre and bake for 25 minutes. Glaze again and finish for 10 more minutes.

T I P If more convenient, use bought pastry. Ready-made comes in a 500 g pack or, if buying ready-rolled, a 375 g pack will do perfectly.

MOUSSAKA WITH NEW POTATOES

Make this when you see the new-season potatoes arriving from Jersey – great flavours with a real rustle of spring.

EASY: *allow 30 minutes to prepare, 30 minutes to bake*

SERVES 6

550 g/1 lb 2 oz new potatoes

2 onions

2 garlic cloves

1 fresh or dried chilli

2 tbsp olive oil

550 g/1 lb 2 oz raw minced lamb

200 g can of tomatoes

1 tbsp chopped fresh mint or 1 tsp
  dried mint

salt and pepper

For the topping:

125 g/4 oz strong hard cheese

2 × 150 ml cartons of Greek
  yogurt

2 medium eggs

salt and pepper

❶ Boil the new potatoes in boiling, salted water, drain and cut in bite-size pieces.

❷ Chop the onions, garlic and chilli finely (can be done in a food processor) and fry in the olive oil for about 5 minutes, till beginning to soften. Add the lamb and brown over a strong heat for about 7 minutes. Drain off any fat and juices in the pan, add the tomatoes and cook for a further 3 minutes, till the tomatoes have broken up. Stir in the mint and season well.

❸ Preheat the oven to 200°C/180°C fan oven/Gas Mark 6. Mix the potatoes and meat and put in a baking dish – pack down firmly.

❹ Whizz the cheese in a processor. Set aside 2 tbsp and to the rest add the yogurt, eggs and seasoning. Pour over the meat, sprinkle with the remaining cheese and bake for about 25–30 minutes, till the topping is set and lightly browned.

POLENTA GNOCCHI

The recipe was inspired by a great book designed for those with an intolerance to wheat (coeliacs) called Great Healthy Food Gluten-free, *by Michael Cox (Carroll and Brown, £12; call the Express Bookshop on 0870 366 6092).*

FOR THE KEEN COOK: *allow 45 minutes; freezes well*

SERVES 4

1 litre/1½ pints milk	150 g/5 oz polenta
1 large onion, peeled and studded	3 egg yolks
with 1–2 cloves	125 g/4 oz parmesan cheese, grated
1 bay leaf	salt and pepper
freshly grated nutmeg	melted butter, for brushing and
a pinch of salt	greasing

1 Lightly grease a baking sheet with a little oil. Pour the milk into a large saucepan, add the onion and bay leaf, nutmeg and salt. Simmer for 10 minutes, rather like making bread sauce, then discard the onion and bay leaf.

2 Measure the polenta and, holding it high above the pan, pour into the hot milk in a slow steady stream, stirring constantly. Continue stirring over a low heat for 10 minutes or as directed on the packet, until it has a thick consistency and pulls away from the sides of the pan. Add a little more milk if the polenta becomes too thick.

3 Remove from the heat and beat in the egg yolks, one at a time. Beat in half the cheese and season well, adding a little more nutmeg if you wish. Turn out on to the baking sheet and spread into an even layer about 1 cm/½-inch thick. Brush with melted butter, then leave for at least 20 minutes to cool – or overnight if convenient.

4 Preheat the oven to 230°C/210°C fan oven/Gas Mark 8. Grease an ovenproof dish with melted butter. Turn the polenta on to a board and cut in 5 cm/2-inch squares. Place them overlapping in the dish, sprinkle with the remaining cheese and bake for about 15 minutes, until nicely browned. Serve with a salad, tossed with a herb and garlic dressing.

MUSTARD PORK
WITH BLACKBERRIES

An adventurous all-in-one meal.

WORTH THE TROUBLE: *allow 1¹/₄ hours*

SERVES 6

1 tbsp fennel seeds	625 g/1¹/₄ lb pork fillet
1 tbsp cumin seeds	2 tbsp Dijon mustard
1 tsp whole black peppercorns	2 tbsp dry white wine
1 tsp dried thyme	400 ml/14 fl oz chicken stock
1 tbsp dry mustard	1 tbsp flour
¹/₂ tsp ground cinnamon	150 g/5 oz fresh blackberries
1 tsp sugar	salt
625 g/1¹/₂ lb baking potatoes, peeled	2 tsp chopped fresh thyme, to
1 tbsp olive oil	garnish

❶ Put the first three ingredients in a dry frying pan and toast over a
medium heat, rolling the pan to keep the seeds moving, for 2 minutes,
then grind in a pestle and mortar or coffee mill. Stir in the thyme,
mustard powder, cinnamon, a teaspoon of salt and sugar.

❷ Preheat the oven to 220°C/200°C fan oven/Gas Mark 7. Cut the potatoes
into thin wedges or 1 cm/¹/₂-inch slices. Toss with the oil and 3 tbsp of
the spice mixture. Spread on a baking sheet and bake for 15 minutes.

❸ Meanwhile, rub the pork with half the Dijon mustard. Sprinkle with a
little salt and 2 tbsp of the spice mixture. Pat on firmly with your hands
and put in a small, oiled roasting pan. Roast for 25 minutes.

❹ Put the pork and potatoes on a board and keep warm. Stir the wine
into the pork roasting tin, scraping up any browned bits. Stir in the stock
and cook for 5–7 minutes, till reduced by half. Whisk together the flour
and 3 tbsp cold water in a bowl, then whisk into the simmering stock
mixture, then add the remaining mustard. Cook till the mixture begins
to thicken, then stir in the blackberries.

❺ Serve slices of pork with sauce and potatoes, sprinkled with thyme.

PORK, MUSHROOM AND PORCINI CASSEROLE

This is a good dinner party dish, because it can be completed in advance.

EASY: *half an hour to get together, 1¹/₂ hours simmering; freezes well*

SERVES 6

25 g/1 oz porcini or other dried mushrooms

1 kg/2 lb pork topside, cut in 2 cm/³/₄-inch cubes

a little seasoned plain flour

a little olive oil

1 onion, chopped

2 garlic cloves, crushed

125 ml/4 fl oz dry white wine

10 juniper berries, crushed

50 ml/2 fl oz red-wine vinegar

1 tbsp chopped fresh marjoram

200 g/7 oz button mushrooms, halved

salt and pepper

❶ Soak the dried mushrooms in 200 ml/8 fl oz of boiling water for 20 minutes. Meanwhile, toss the pork in the flour. Heat a little olive oil in a large ovenproof casserole and cook the pork, in batches, till golden – about 5 minutes per batch. Add more oil if necessary and remove the pork from the pan as it is done. Add 1 tbsp oil to casserole and cook the onion and garlic for 5 minutes, till soft.

❷ Stir in the wine and whisk in all the browned bits from the sides and bottom of the pan, bring to the boil and stir in the pork, juniper berries, dried mushrooms and their liquor, half the vinegar and the marjoram. Season and bring to a simmer. Cook for an hour, covered.

❸ Add the button mushrooms, stir well and cook for a further 30 minutes, or till tender. Stir in remaining vinegar, season to taste and serve.

PRAWN AND COCONUT CURRY

This recipe is from Thane Prince, who runs the Aldeburgh Cookery School in Suffolk. She describes it as being 'in the Goan style', meaning that it is fairly dry and not too hot. I have adapted the recipe slightly to use fresh ginger, rather than ginger purée, which comes in small jars but can be difficult to find.

EASY AND DIFFERENT: *15 minutes to prepare, 10 minutes to cook*

SERVES 4

75 g/3 oz desiccated coconut

300 ml/½ pint milk

2 tbsp oil

a bunch of spring onions, chopped roughly

2 garlic cloves, chopped

2.5 cm/1-inch cube of fresh ginger, chopped (see Tip)

3 tsp curry paste

juice of ½ a lemon

a good pinch of caster sugar

450 g/15 oz cooked prawns (thawed and drained if frozen)

a knob of butter

salt and pepper

a handful of fresh parsley or basil, chopped or shredded, to serve

❶ Pour the milk over the coconut, stir and set aside.

❷ Heat the oil in a large frying pan and, when hot, add the spring onions, garlic and ginger. Sizzle, stirring often, for 2–3 minutes, then add the curry paste and cook 2–3 minutes longer. Add the coconut, lemon juice, sugar and seasoning and cook for 2–3 minutes.

❸ The sauce at this point will be thick and fairly dry. Just before you want to eat, stir in the prawns for just a minute or two, till hot, then melt in the butter, stirring gently. If you overcook the dish at this point, the prawns will become dry and the sauce too wet, so serve immediately with the herbs scattered on top.

> **TIP** 🥣 You don't need to peel ginger before chopping or grating it.

SALMON FILLETS TOPPED
WITH HERBY BREADCRUMBS

*From the Isle of Wight comes this dead simple recipe, created by
Amy Willcock, an American cook who runs courses at the George
Hotel in Yarmouth.*

EASY: *allow 30 minutes from start to finish*

SERVES 4

4 fresh salmon fillets

**4 tbsp fresh breadcrumbs (about
    2 slices of bread, crusts off)**

2 tbsp chopped fresh herbs

**2 rashers of smoked bacon,
    chopped finely**

2 tbsp olive oil

1 Preheat the oven to 200°C/180°C fan oven/Gas Mark 6. Lightly grease
a baking sheet and put the salmon on it. In a bowl, combine the remaining
ingredients and press on to the salmon.

2 Cook for 13–15 minutes. Serve with new potatoes and a fresh green
vegetable.

T I P Amy is an Aga fan and, if you are too, cook this recipe
at the bottom of the roasting oven for 5 minutes, then move to the
top of the oven for a further 5–8 minutes.

SARAH CROCKETT'S DEVILLED CHICKEN

This recipe was given to me by my GP's wife, who says everyone always asks her for the recipe. I can see why. The spices can be varied but use enough to make a good impact. After all, you are aiming for a devilish effect.

EASY: *allow 50 minutes, including 30–40 minutes baking*

SERVES 4

1 tbsp olive oil	4 tsp ground cumin
4 chicken breasts	4 tbsp tomato ketchup
284 ml carton of double cream	1 tsp Tabasco sauce
1 tbsp mustard powder	salt and pepper
1 tbsp paprika	

1 Preheat the oven to 180°C/160°C fan oven/Gas Mark 4. Brown the chicken in the oil, allowing 3 minutes per side and put in a roasting tin or ovenproof casserole.

2 Mix the cream and seasonings, plus salt and pepper to taste, and pour over the chicken. Bake for 30–40 minutes, till cooked through.

T I P In recent taste comparisons, Waitrose's ketchup scooped top points. Heinz remains a popular choice, however, and is thankfully free of many of the nasty artificial ingredients that some ketchups contain.

SMOKED SALMON
CASSEROLE

*This is in no way a formal dish but, when you have hungry guests
and you're looking for something yummy and practical, it's just the
thing. Also makes an outstanding brunch.*

EASY AND DELICIOUSLY RICH: *allow 20 minutes to make (in
advance if you wish), 30 minutes to bake*

SERVES 4 – 6

375 g/12 oz small broccoli florets,
   plunged into boiling water for a
   couple of minutes till just tender
   and then drained
10 spring onions, chopped
250 g/8 oz smoked salmon slices,
   cut in wide strips
250 g/8 oz Cheddar cheese, grated
200 g tub of chilled cream cheese,
   cut in rough cubes

To finish:
8 large eggs
450 ml/16 fl oz milk
150 g packet of pancake mix
   (such as Bisquick)
¼ tsp salt
¼ tsp pepper

❶ Butter a 33 × 23 cm/13- × 9-inch baking dish. Arrange the broccoli
and half the spring onions, sprinkle with salmon, cheese, cream cheese
and remaining onions. This can be done a day ahead and refrigerated.

❷ Preheat the oven to 190°C/170°C fan oven/Gas Mark 5. Mix the eggs,
milk, pancake mix, salt and pepper in a blender till smooth, then pour
over the salmon mixture. Bake for 30 minutes till just set in the centre.
Cool for 10 minutes before serving.

> **TIP** 🥣 Any pancake or waffle mix will do for this recipe, but
> do not choose one that is pre-sweetened.

SPICED VENISON CASSEROLE

Venison is the meat of the moment, being less high in fat than beef but quite as tender and mouthwatering. This autumn casserole showcases it perfectly.

FANCY AND WORTH IT: *start a day ahead, a good 2 hours to cook*

SERVES 8: FREEZES WELL

1.25 kg/3 lb venison, either a haunch
or stewing, cut in 2.5 cm/1-inch
cubes

For the marinade:

2 tbsp olive oil

125 g/4 oz pancetta or smoked
streaky bacon, chopped

2 onions, sliced

2 garlic cloves, crushed

2 celery sticks

1 large carrot

2 bay leaves

1 strip of orange zest about
2.5 × 8 cm/1 × 3 inches

2 cinnamon sticks

4 cloves

1 tsp ground allspice

4 tbsp brandy

300 ml/½ pint red wine

salt and pepper

To finish:

1 tbsp olive oil

300 ml/½ pint stock

25 g/1 oz butter

12 shallots, peeled

12 small mushrooms, trimmed

240 g can of chestnuts, drained

1 tbsp pomegranate molasses or
redcurrant jelly

salt and pepper

❶ Make the marinade by heating the oil and frying the pancetta, onions, garlic, celery and carrot for 10 minutes over a brisk heat till golden. Put in a large casserole with the other marinade ingredients and seasoning and allow to cool. Add the venison, cover with cling film and leave for 12 hours at room temperature, or up to 48 hours in the fridge, turning occasionally.

❷ To cook, pick the meat out of the marinade, reserving the marinade, and dry first in a sieve over the bowl so none of the precious juices are wasted, then on kitchen paper. Heat the remaining oil and, in a frying pan, quickly fry the venison pieces (in batches if necessary) till browned, about 3 minutes. Return to the casserole as they cook.

❸ Add the reserved marinade and stock to the casserole. Now bring the meat and marinade to a simmer and cook in the oven, covered, at 160°C/140°C fan oven/Gas Mark 3 for about 2 hours, stirring from time to time, till tender.

❹ Meanwhile, heat the butter and fry the shallots till tender – about 10 minutes. Remove and add to the casserole for the last hour, then fry the mushrooms in the same pan for 5 minutes till brown, and add the chestnuts for a further 2 minutes. Add to the casserole 30 minutes before it is cooked.

❺ Check the seasoning and add the molasses or jelly to add a sweet and sour note. Classic accompaniments are triangles of fried bread or baked potatoes.

T I P This dish is even better made 2–3 days ahead of eating, then reheated at 180°C/160°C fan oven/Gas Mark 4 for 30 minutes.

SPINACH AND FETA PIE

Vegetarians tend to get a rough ride at Christmas and New Year, so here is a special centrepiece to make for them. It is a variation on the Greek dish spanakopitta; if you have leftovers it freezes very well, or divide the mixture in two and freeze one for another time

WORTH THE TROUBLE: *takes 2¹/₂ hours in all, including 1¹/₂ hours baking*

SERVES 6

750 g/1¹/₂ lb fresh spinach, washed and tough stems discarded (or frozen)

250 g/8 oz swiss chard, washed (optional, see Tip)

50 ml/2 fl oz olive oil

1 small onion, chopped finely

125 g/4 oz feta cheese, roughly crumbled

125 g/4 oz cottage cheese

a good handful of finely chopped fresh parsley

2 tbsp finely chopped fresh dill

1 tbsp lemon juice

a pinch of grated nutmeg

1 large egg, beaten

75 g/3 oz melted butter

half a 400g packet of filo pastry (six sheets), defrosted

salt and pepper

❶ Cook the spinach by putting handfuls of leaves in a large pan, tossing with tongs, then adding more handfuls, till they are all in and partially wilted. Drain and let cool – this will take a few minutes – then squeeze out as much liquid as possible. Coarsely chop and put in a large bowl. If using frozen, simply defrost.

❷ If using chard, tear off the stems, chop them and set aside. Cook the leaves in the same way as the spinach, draining and chopping when cool. As for the stems, put half the olive oil in a dry pan (you can use the same one as for the spinach, wiped out) and fry the stems for 2 minutes. Add the onion and cook for 2 more minutes.

❸ Add the chard, if using, and onion, to the spinach with the feta, cottage cheese, parsley, dill, lemon juice and nutmeg. Season well and stir in the egg.

4 Preheat the oven to 180°C/160°C fan oven/Gas Mark 4. Mix the butter with the remaining oil. Lightly grease a 20 cm/8-inch square dish, or equivalent round dish.

5 Keep your supply of filo sheets covered with a damp cloth while you are working. Take one sheet, butter it, fold over buttered-side in and butter what is now the top. Repeat twice, until you have used three sheets and now have six layers. Put this stack in the baking dish.

6 Spread the spinach mixture evenly on top. Repeat with the remaining pastry and put on top of the filling. Trim the top pastry layer to fit the lower, then crimp together. Lightly score the top into 6 using a sharp knife and drizzle over any remaining butter.

7 Bake for 1½ hours, or until golden and crisp. Leave for 10 minutes before serving.

T I P S Swiss chard is a great vegetable but, if you can't get it, up the spinach to 1 kg/2 lb.

The dish can be refrigerated at end of step 6 and kept overnight.

FILLETS OF SOLE
IN HORSERADISH

This is a very special, classic lunch recipe of country-house origin.
Sole fillets are extremely expensive, so cook them with care.

NOT DIFFICULT: *1 hour to prepare, 8 minutes to cook; can be made a day ahead*

SERVES 4 AS A REAL TREAT

8 fillets of sole	**4 dsp white-wine vinegar**
300 ml/½ pint milk	**1½ dsp granulated sugar**
For the sauce:	**salt**
2 dsp grated horseradish, either	**142 ml carton of double cream**
fresh or bottled	**plenty of fresh chives and parsley,**
1 tsp dry mustard	**to serve**
1 tsp ground white pepper	

❶ Preheat the oven to 180°C/160°C fan oven/Gas Mark 4. Lay the fish in a heatproof dish in one layer. Bring the milk to the boil, pour over and then put the dish in the oven for 7–8 minutes only, till the fish is just tender. It is crucial not to overcook the fish; it will finish cooking as it cools, during which time cover loosely with foil.

❷ Make the sauce by mixing the first six ingredients. It will taste very strong, and so it should, but check it has enough salt; it needs plenty. Stir in the cream and leave for an hour – it will thicken slightly.

❸ To serve, gently pull each fillet in half and lay in a large dish, preferably not overlapping. Spoon over the sauce; if the fish does overlap, spoon some sauce between the pieces of fish. Shake the dish so the sauce settles a little. Chop the herbs very, very finely (the cook who taught me this virtually powdered them) and sprinkle all over like a green blanket. Refrigerate till half an hour before serving, accompanied by a little buttered brown bread.

SPANISH-STYLE BAKED FISH

Here is a very straightforward fish recipe that suits relaxed entertaining.
It looks great and doesn't traumatise the cook!

E A S Y: *allow 15 minutes to make, 1 hour in the oven*

S E R V E S   6

1.05 kg/2¼ lb waxy new potatoes, such as Charlotte, sliced thinly

4 garlic cloves, sliced thinly

2 large red onions, cut in wedges

2 red peppers, de-seeded and cut in chunks

2 yellow peppers, de-seeded and cut in chunks

5 tbsp extra-virgin olive oil

150 g/5 oz black olives

6 bay leaves

6 × 175 g/6 oz thick-cut haddock or cod fillets

juice of 1 small lemon

150 g fresh pesto sauce

salt and freshly ground black pepper

lemon wedges, to serve

❶ Preheat the oven to 200°C/fan oven 180°C/Gas Mark 6. Pat the sliced potatoes dry with kitchen paper and then toss with the garlic, red onions, peppers and 4 tablespoons of the oil in a large shallow roasting tin or ovenproof dish. Roast for 45 minutes, until the vegetables are beginning to soften and turn golden around the edges.

❷ Scatter the black olives and bay leaves over the vegetables, then sit the fish on top in one layer.

❸ Mix the remaining oil, the lemon juice and pesto together and spoon over the fish fillets. Season with a little salt and plenty of ground black pepper. Roast in the oven for 15 minutes. Serve straight away, with extra wedges of lemon and a crisp green salad.

T I P ⬭ Fine fish – the fresher the better – will make a real difference to this summery stew.

CHICKEN TALEGGIO

This is a very simple recipe for stuffed chicken breasts, suitable for entertaining or a special family supper. The recipe was very carefully worked out in the Good Food *test kitchen, which each month creates a recipe for total beginners – of which this is an example. The fun part is that we actually invite a beginner in to the test kitchen to see if and where they go wrong. (Once our beginner's recipe was for a soufflé, and the cookery editor just managed to prevent the beginner from adding the egg whites before they'd been beaten!)*

STRAIGHTFORWARD: *allow 40 minutes to an hour*

SERVES 4

4 × 175 g/6 oz boneless, skinless chicken breasts	15 g packet of fresh sage leaves
	2 tbsp olive oil
about 150 g/5 oz taleggio cheese, cut lengthways from the block	a knob of butter
	200 ml/7 fl oz chicken stock
4 very thin slices of Parma ham (prosciutto di Parma)	4 tbsp double cream
	salt and freshly ground black pepper

❶ Flatten all four chicken breasts by putting them between sheets of clingfilm and beating with a rolling pin until they are thin and relatively even. Put them on a plate. Cut the taleggio lengthways into four equal slices. Put one piece of chicken, flattened-side up and with one of its short sides facing you, on a board. Grind a little black pepper evenly on the chicken, then put one slice of taleggio lengthways in the centre.

❷ Starting at the short end nearest to you, roll the chicken away from you into a sausage shape, with the cheese enclosed in the centre. Put the roll on a plate and repeat with the remaining chicken and cheese.

3 Put one slice of prosciutto lengthways on the board. Arrange four sage leaves along its length, spacing them out evenly and at right angles to the prosciutto. Lay one chicken roll, seam-side down, at the end nearest to you and roll the prosciutto loosely around the chicken. Repeat to make four rolls altogether, setting them aside on the plate as you complete each one.

4 Put the oil and butter in a large frying pan and set the pan on the hob over a medium–high heat for a minute or so until the butter has melted and is foaming. Lay the chicken rolls in the pan and cook for 12 minutes. Turn them over from time to time and baste them with the hot oil and butter mixture (this helps them cook through). At the end of cooking, the prosciutto should be golden brown on all sides of each roll and any exposed chicken should be white, not pink. Remove the rolls with a slotted spoon and set them aside on a plate.

5 Pour the chicken stock into the pan, increase the heat to high and stir vigorously with a wooden spoon as the stock sizzles. Scrape the spoon over the bottom and around the sides of the pan to dislodge any bits of sediment. This is called deglazing.

6 Spoon in the cream and stir until it is evenly mixed with the stock, then taste for seasoning and add some salt and pepper if you think the sauce needs it. Return the chicken to the pan and simmer for 2 minutes, shaking the pan and spooning the sauce on top of the chicken so the rolls become evenly coated in sauce. Serve on warmed plates, garnished with little sprigs of sage and accompanied by boiled new potatoes and a fresh seasonal vegetable such as green beans.

> **T I P** 🥄 Taleggio is a soft Italian cheese. If you can't find it, use Brie.

CARBONNADE FLAMANDE

Prepare-ahead cooking of this kind suits me down to the ground, enabling me to do the work as and when I feel like it. It is also worth noting that this recipe reheats and freezes perfectly.

EASY AND DELICIOUS: *allow 3 hours – begin a day ahead; can be reheated or frozen*

SERVES 4 – 6

625 g/1¼ lb topside of beef, cut in small steaks about 7.5–10 cm/ 3 – 4 inches across

2 large onions, sliced

2 medium carrots, sliced

a bouquet garni

450–600 ml/¾–1 pint beer

3 tbsp oil

about 50 g/2 oz plain flour

2 tsp brown sugar

1 tsp smooth French mustard

salt and pepper

❶ Put the beef in a dish with the onions, carrots and bouquet garni and cover with the beer. Leave to marinate in a cool place or the fridge for 24 hours.

❷ Preheat the oven to 150°C/130°C fan oven/Gas Mark 2. Heat 2 tbsp of the oil in a frying pan. Remove the meat from the marinade and dip in about three-quarters of the flour, which you have seasoned with salt and pepper. Fry the pieces until brown on both sides and set aside.

❸ Remove onions from marinade with a slotted spoon and fry till golden. Set aside.

❹ In an ovenproof casserole, layer up the meat and onions. Put the remaining oil into the frying pan and sprinkle 1 tbsp of flour into it. Cook until pale brown, then start whisking in the marinade (including the carrot slices) until thick and boiling. Stir in the brown sugar and mustard and pour over the meat, then bake for 2½–3 hours.

GOAT'S CHEESE SOUFFLÉ

This is a soufflé for beginners. It was featured in Good Food *magazine with a promise we would refund your ingredients if the recipe went wrong – and not a single cook took us up on our offer.*

FUN TO MAKE: *allow 30 minutes to make, 40 minutes in the oven*

SERVES 4

50 g/2 oz butter, plus a little extra soft butter for greasing the dish	1 bay leaf
	50 g/2 oz plain flour
4 eggs	50 g/2 oz parmesan cheese,
125 g/4 oz firm goat's cheese, with rind	grated
	15 g packet of fresh chives
300 ml/½ pint milk	salt and pepper

❶ Put a heavy baking sheet in the oven and preheat to 190°C/fan oven 180°C/Gas Mark 5. Grease a 1.2-litre/2-pint soufflé dish with soft butter. Separate the eggs. Finely chop the goat's cheese, including the rind.

❷ Put the milk, bay leaf, butter and flour together in a pan. Bring just to the boil, whisking vigorously all the time with a whisk until smooth and very thick.

❸ Remove from the heat and discard the bay leaf. Whisk in the two cheeses, reserving 1 tablespoon of the parmesan, then the egg yolks, one at a time. Snip the chives into the sauce, season and set aside.

❹ Whisk the egg whites till stiff. Using a wooden spoon, stir two spoonfuls of the egg whites into the cheese sauce in the pan. Using a spatula or large metal spoon, gently fold in the remaining egg whites until evenly mixed.

❺ Pour the mixture into the prepared soufflé dish, sprinkle with the reserved parmesan, then make a deep groove in the mixture by running your thumb around the inside edge. Get out the hot baking sheet, stand the soufflé on it and put in the oven for 35–40 minutes. To test if the soufflé is done, slowly open the oven door and give the dish a gentle shake – the soufflé should wobble slightly. If it wobbles too much, bake it for a further few minutes. Serve straightaway.

SPICED CHICKEN
WITH COUSCOUS

This spice mixture is a great larder standby – you can rub it on grills, roasts or (best of all) barbecues. If you don't have garlic powder – and I use it very rarely – a little chopped garlic will make a perfect substitute, but this will have to be added fresh each time.

EASY: *allow 40 minutes*

SERVES 4

For the spice rub:

2½ tsp paprika

1 tsp dried thyme

¾ tsp garlic powder

½ tsp dried oregano

½ tsp salt

¼ tsp black pepper

a good pinch of cayenne pepper

For the chicken:

4 skinless, boneless chicken breast fillets

2 tbsp oil

1 small onion, chopped

1 garlic clove, chopped

175 g/6 oz couscous

250 ml/8 fl oz boiling chicken stock

198 g can of sweetcorn, drained

2 tbsp chopped fresh coriander or parsley

1 tbsp lime juice

❶ Combine the rub ingredients in a shallow dish and rub all over the chicken.

❷ Heat half the oil in a large non-stick pan over medium heat. Add the chicken and cook for 5 minutes on each side, till done. Remove from pan and keep warm.

❸ Heat the remaining oil and fry the onion and garlic for 1 minute. Stir in the couscous and stock and bring to the boil. Remove from the heat. Stir in the sweetcorn, cover and leave for 5 minutes until the liquid is absorbed. Stir in the parsley and lime juice.

❹ Serve the chicken sliced on a bed of couscous.

chapter 7

DASHING DESSERTS

Have you noticed that many people say sniffily that they don't eat desserts, then proceed to tuck in as if they'd never tasted anything so delicious? I think these people are in truth dessert-starved; they deprive themselves of this treat only to fall upon it like manna once they taste what they've been missing.

I happen to love desserts, and this is a small selection of my favourites. They vary in difficulty, ranging from the homely to the dazzling, but they all reward your efforts with something delectable and tempting.

APPLE, APRICOT AND GINGER CRUMBLE

Crumbles may not be haute cuisine but I can't think of any dessert I would rather eat on a winter's evening. In this recipe I have given the crumble a nice oaty crunch, and the spices add extra warmth. Some people prefer more crumble to fruit, or the other way round: this is a happy medium so, if you wish, you can take it in your preferred direction.

EASY: *allow 1¹/4 hours, including 50–60 minutes baking; freezes well*

SERVES 4 – 6

2 medium Bramleys, about 375 g/ 12 oz in total

125 g/4 oz organic dried apricots, sliced (see Tip)

2 pieces of stem ginger, chopped, plus 1 tbsp syrup from the jar

1 tsp ground mixed spice

50 g/2 oz brown sugar, mixed with 2 tsp cornflour

grated zest and juice of 1 orange

For the crumble:

150 g/5 oz plain flour

75 g/3 oz rolled oats

75 g/3 oz butter

50 g/2 oz caster sugar

1 tsp ground cinnamon or ground mixed spice

❶ Preheat the oven to 190°C/170°C fan oven/Gas Mark 5. Peel, core and quarter the apples and slice each quarter into 4 or 5 pieces. Mix the fruit and ginger and toss with the spice, sugar and cornflour and orange zest and arrange in a 1-litre/1³/4-pint baking dish. Sprinkle with the orange juice.

❷ Rub the butter into the flour and oats, then stir in the sugar and spice. Spoon over the fruit and bake for 50 minutes to an hour, covering with foil if the top gets too brown.

> **TIP** 🥣 Of all the organic products on sale, the one that is most different from its non-organic counterpart is organic dried apricots. Though dingy in colour they have the most wonderful flavour – once you taste it you will be converted forever.

BÊTE NOIRE

This is one of those intensely rich chocolate confections, to serve in very small slices.

TAKES SOME CARE BUT ULTRA-SPECIAL: *allow 25 minutes to make, 45–50 minutes to cook; freezes well*

SERVES 12

125 g/4 oz caster sugar

275 g/9 oz best dark chocolate, preferably specifying 70% cocoa solids on the label

125 g/4 oz butter, chopped and left to come to room temperature

3 eggs

2 tbsp caster sugar

1 vanilla pod, halved lengthways

a little cocoa powder, sifted

❶ Preheat the oven to 160°C/140°C fan oven/Gas Mark 3. Base-line a 20 cm/8-inch cake tin (not loose-based) with baking parchment and grease well; stand in a deep roasting tin and put a kettle on to boil. Combine 50 ml/2 fl oz of water and the first lot of sugar in a small pan and stir until dissolved. Remove from heat and stir in the chocolate: stir till smooth, then add butter and stir till just melted. Transfer to a large bowl.

❷ Beat the eggs, remaining sugar and vanilla seeds (scraped from the pod) with an electric mixer for a full 5–7 minutes, till tripled in volume and mousse-like. Fold one-third of this mixture into the chocolate, then the rest. Stop the moment it is combined.

❸ Pour the mixture into the baking tin and pour enough boiling water into the roasting tin to come halfway up the sides. Bake for 45–50 minutes, until risen in the centre and slightly domed (it will still feel slightly soft to the touch – this is correct). Remove from the roasting tin of water to cool and then refrigerate for 5 hours, or overnight, till firm.

❹ Turn out of the tin and dust with cocoa. Cut in thin slices with a knife you have dipped in boiling water and dried. Serve with rasperries and cream.

BROWN SUGAR BUTTERNUT SQUASH PIE

This recipe will be made all the more sumptuous by choosing the right sugar. I always choose muscovado by preference – either the dark or light varieties – as the flavour is so much better. If you can't find this, the word to look for is 'unrefined' as this always indicates a better-tasting product. This is a really lovely sweet tart made with butternut squashes – those rather hard-skinned long-shaped mini-pumpkins you can get most of the year. It is very much like a subtle pumpkin pie, and has the advantage of not needing to prebake the pastry.

A REAL TREAT: *1¹/₄ hours to prepare, 40 minutes to cook*

SERVES 8 – 10

For the crust:

23 cm/9-inch pastry case, made with 175 g/6 oz plain flour, 125 g/4 oz butter, ¹/₂ tsp each of salt and sugar and 2 tbsp water to bind

For the butternut squash:

2 butternut squashes

40 g/1¹/₂ oz butter

50 g/2 oz dark muscovado sugar

3 tbsp orange juice

For the custard:

75 g/3 oz dark muscovado sugar

3 large eggs

142 ml carton of double cream

¹/₂ tsp each of ground allspice, ginger, cinnamon and salt

❶ Line the pie dish or flan tin with the pastry and chill till needed.

❷ Preheat the oven to 200°C/180°C fan oven/Gas Mark 6. Halve and remove strings and seeds from the chubby end of each butternut squash but do not peel. Dot with the butter and sugar, drizzle with orange juice and then put, cut-side up, into a baking dish and bake for 40–45 minutes, till the flesh is tender. When cool enough to handle, drain off the liquid, peel off the skin and purée the flesh in a food processor till smooth. You should have about 500 g/1 lb. (If you have substantially more you can serve it as a vegetable, turn it into soup or use as a pasta sauce, mixed with herbs, ricotta and parmesan. The purée can be frozen.)

❸ Turn the oven down to 190°C/170°C fan oven/Gas Mark 5. Put in a baking sheet to heat. Mix the purée with the muscovado sugar, eggs, cream and spices and whisk till smooth. Pour into the chilled crust, stand on the baking sheet and bake for 40 minutes, till the filling has puffed up and feels just firm to the touch. Serve warm.

T I P It is quite fun to make pastry decorations for this pie. To do this cut out shapes – leaves or other motifs – lay on baking parchment, sprinkle generously with sugar and bake for 12 minutes at 180°C/160°C fan oven/Gas Mark 4. Lay on the pie just before serving. The sugar really makes a difference, and turns the leaves from mere decorations into extra treats in their own right.

CRANBERRY AND ALMOND TART

NOT DIFFICULT: *allow about 2 hours, including 45 minutes baking*

SERVES 8

For the pastry:

125 g/4 oz plain flour

25 g/1 oz self-raising flour

1 tbsp icing sugar

75 g/3 oz butter

1 egg, separated

a pinch of salt

2–3 tbsp water

For the cranberries:

375 g/12 oz fresh cranberries

juice of 1 orange

50 g/2 oz caster sugar

2 tbsp rum or whisky

For the topping:

75 g/3 oz butter

150 g/5 oz caster sugar

2 medium eggs

grated zest of 1 orange

150 g/5 oz ground almonds

25 g/1 oz plain flour

icing sugar, for dusting

❶ Make the pastry by combining the flours and icing sugar, rubbing in the butter and mixing with the yolk of the egg (save the white) and enough water to combine (can be done in a processor). Leave to rest for 30 minutes in the fridge. Roll out and line a 23 cm/9-inch flan tin. Rest again for 15 minutes. Preheat the oven to 190°C/170°C fan oven/Gas Mark 5. Brush the flan case lightly with some of the egg white, set on a baking sheet and bake for about 15–17 minutes, till golden. Turn the oven down to 180°C/160°C fan oven/Gas Mark 4.

❷ Meanwhile, wash and cook the cranberries with the orange juice for about 10 minutes, till soft and juicy. Stir in the sugar and alcohol.

❸ For the topping, cream the butter and sugar with the orange zest. Add the eggs slowly. Fold in the almonds and flour.

❹ When ready to bake, put the cranberries into the pastry case, spread the topping over, then bake for 45 minutes. If the topping browns too quickly, cover with foil and turn oven down to 160°C/140°C fan oven/Gas Mark 3. Serve cool or warm with cream, greek yogurt or crème fraîche.

DRIED APRICOTS
IN MARSALA

I am no great fan of fresh apricots, finding them furry on the outside and a little tough and tart when you get inside. Make them into jam, though, and I am their number-one fan.

I was introduced to dried apricots many years ago by my late friend Diana Gordon. Diana was a very fine musician and we met through my best-ever piano teacher, who was a mutual friend. I think musicians make very good cooks, and Diana had it all to a fine art. This is what Diana did with dried apricots. Sometimes she'd serve them plain, sometimes as a fool.

EASY: *no time to prepare, 15 minutes to cook; keeps well for 3–4 days*

SERVES 6

250 g/8 oz dried organic apricots

1 vanilla pod

100 ml/3½ fl oz water

100 ml/3½ fl oz marsala

whipped cream, to serve

❶ Split the vanilla pod down the centre. Put everything in a pan and simmer for 10–15 minutes until the apricots are nice and soft. Serve in a small glass bowl, warm or cool, with cream; leave the vanilla pod in to serve (it looks pretty) but, after eating the apricots, wash it well and store it in sugar to make your own perfumed vanilla sugar.

> **T I P** 🥄 You can make this into a simple, pleasantly textured fool by liquidising when cold and folding into a 284 ml carton of whipping cream, lightly whipped, or half whipping cream softly whipped with half greek yogurt. Serve with ratafias or crumble some over the top. The same trick works for prunes.

GOAT'S CHEESE
CHEESECAKE

I first tasted this recipe in a competition I was judging, and the competitor (who won, incidentally) told me it was an adaptation of a recipe by that inspiring recipe writer Nigel Slater. The texture of the pastry and flavour of the filling are both excellent, and I have made it several times since.

The pastry is handy in that it doesn't need rolling out, nor lining with baking beans and all that palaver.

FRESH, FUN AND DELICIOUS: *30 minutes to prepare, 50 minutes to cook; best served very fresh*

SERVES 8

For the pastry:

250 g/8 oz plain flour

125 g/4 oz butter, cut up

1½ tbsp caster sugar

grated zest of ½ lemon

½ tsp vanilla extract

1–2 tbsp water

For the filling:

300 g/10 oz fresh soft goat's cheese

200 g/7 oz mascarpone

75 g/3 oz caster sugar

25 g/1 oz butter, melted

grated zest and juice of 1 lemon

2 tbsp ground almonds

a few drops of vanilla extract

1 large egg, separated

For the topping:

200 g tub of crème fraîche

1 tbsp caster sugar

125 g/4 oz fresh fruit of your choice, sliced (optional)

❶ Make the pastry by putting all ingredients in a processor. Whizz until evenly blended (add the extra water if it looks dry), then gather in your hands and press lightly into a ball. Take a 20 cm/8-inch, loose-based fluted flan tin and lay thin slices of the pastry all over the base and round the sides; press with the flat of your hand and your fingers until you have a smooth pastry base all round. Put in the freezer for 30 minutes.

❷ Preheat the oven to 200°C/180°C fan oven/Gas Mark 6. Put the pastry case on a baking sheet and bake for 12 minutes until lightly golden and dryish – no need to line the base with baking beans and so on. Remove from oven and turn down to 160°C/140°C fan oven/Gas Mark 3 – it is easy to forget to do this, so do it now.

❸ Meanwhile, mix all the filling ingredients except 25 g/1 oz of the sugar and the egg white till smooth. Whisk the egg white till stiff, adding the sugar towards the end. Fold the egg white into the cream mixture and pour into the still-hot pastry case. It will puff during cooking so do not overfill.

❹ Bake for 50 minutes till a rich gold. Turn off the oven and leave to cool undisturbed, opening the door slightly after 15 minutes. The cheesecake will crack.

❺ When cool, spread the top with the crème fraîche mixed with the sugar and, if you wish, fruit.

T I P Use the soft goat's cheese for this, the whiter and fresher the better.

KATE'S ORANGE JELLY

This jelly, which is simplicity itself, is perfect for a dinner party and my friend Kate Birk, whose household is something of a maelstrom, what with busy lives and daughters galore, invented it herself. If you are of a nervous disposition, leave to set in a pretty bowl and there is no need to turn it out.

EASY: *5 minutes to prepare, 10 minutes to segment the orange, leave overnight to set*

SERVES 6

a packet of orange jelly

150 ml/¼ pint freshly squeezed
   orange juice (from a carton
   is fine)

2–4 tbsp Drambuie

2 oranges, segmented (see Tip)

❶ Put the jelly in a measuring jug and pour over boiling water up to the 150 ml/¼ pint mark. Stir to dissolve. Add orange juice and Drambuie, then top up with boiling water to just less than 600 ml/1 pint.

❷ Allow to cool, then refrigerate until at the point of setting – about 1½ hours. Stir in the orange segments, pour into a mould of a little more than 600 ml/1 pint capacity and leave to set overnight. Turn out and serve with whipped cream.

TIP Segmenting oranges is a bit fiddly but worth the trouble. Peel the oranges with a knife, discarding all pith. Holding the orange in one hand and using a sawing motion with a small serrated knife in your other hand, cut each individual segment free from its fibrous compartment. Discard the fibrous membranes.

LEMON POSSET

This incredibly simple recipe was given to me and my colleague by the best caterer I have ever known, Lorna Wing. Lorna, now a consultant to the party world rather than actually running round fixing parties for the rich and famous, has the most exquisite taste and, like every great cook, knows that simple things are the best.

VERY EASY: *allow 10 minutes to make, chill overnight*

SERVES 6

600 ml/1 pint double cream

150 g/5 oz caster sugar

juice of 2 lemons

amaretti or other biscuits, to serve

❶ Tip the cream and sugar into a pan and slowly bring to the boil, stirring to dissolve the sugar, then boil for exactly 3 minutes. Remove from heat and whisk in the lemon juice.

❷ Pour into small glasses and leave to cool. Chill overnight – they will lightly set.

> **TIP** ☺ To make this remarkable dessert, follow the instructions carefully – the timing of the boiling of the cream is critical.

LUSCIOUS LEMON TART

There are many ways to make a lemon tart and everyone seems to like theirs different. This version has an intense lemon filling – in fact a lemon curd filling – and is based on egg rather than cream. Freeze the leftover egg whites for use when you next make meringues; three of them could certainly be used for Chocolate and Walnut Cake (page 174).

REQUIRES A LITTLE CARE: *allow 40 minutes if using bought pastry*

SERVES 8

20 cm/8-inch tart shell, prebaked (see Tip)

6 large egg yolks, plus 2 whole eggs

125 g/4 oz caster sugar

grated zest of 2 lemons, juice of 4 lemons

a pinch of salt

25 g/1 oz butter

3 tbsp double cream

1 Preheat the oven to 190°C/170°C fan oven/Gas Mark 5. If you bake the tart case in advance, reheat for 5 minutes before filling with lemon mixture, as it needs to be hot at this point.

2 Mix the yolks and whole eggs, then add the sugar, lemon juice, zest and salt. Transfer to a saucepan with the butter and cook until the mixture thickens slightly – about 5 minutes. Do not boil. Strain, stir in the cream and pour into the warm tart shell.

3 Bake for 10 to 15 minutes, till the filling is shiny and opaque and the centre still wobbles gently when shaken. Cool for 45 minutes, then the tart is ready to serve.

T I P Either buy 350 g/10 oz of ready-made shortcrust or sweet shortcrust pastry, or make your own using 175 g/6 oz of plain flour, 75 g/3 oz of butter, 1 tbsp of icing sugar and about 2 tbsp of cold water.

MOCHA HEDGEHOG PUDDING

This is a doddle of a dessert: a rich biscuity mixture is enriched with coffee and chocolate, left to set and then covered with cream. Stick nuts all over it, hedgehog style, and you've a sumptuous dinner-party dessert. EASY: *10 minutes to make, no time to cook – chill overnight*

SERVES 8–10 (QUITE RICH)

125 g/4 oz butter, cut in pieces

125 g/4 oz sugar

300 ml/½ pint strong black coffee

1 egg, beaten

3 tbsp cocoa powder

175 g/6 oz rich tea biscuits (18 biscuits)

125 g/4 oz ground almonds

For the decoration:

250 ml/8 fl oz double cream

1 tbsp Kahlua or coffee liqueur

25 g/1 oz flaked almonds, toasted

❶ Melt the butter and sugar with the coffee in a medium pan. Cool slightly, stir into the egg and heat for 1–2 minutes, stirring. It will start to thicken slightly but do not allow to boil. Stir in the cocoa.

❷ Break the biscuits into rough chunks (each biscuit into about 6 pieces) and add to the sugar and butter mixture, with the ground almonds. Mix together and leave for 10 minutes. Meanwhile, line a 600 ml/1-pint pudding bowl with a piece of plastic film. Put the pudding mixture into the bowl, allow to cool, cover and then chill for at least 6 hours, or overnight.

❸ Before serving, whip the cream with the liqueur to soft peaks. Invert the pudding on to a serving plate (run a knife round the inside of the bowl if necessary, to loosen) and peel away the plastic lining. Decorate with the nuts stuck on hedgehog style.

SAUCY LEMON PUDDING

You can't beat the old favourites and here I would like to remind you of that gorgeous melt-in-the-mouth lemon pudding that separates as you cook it, into a layer of sponge and a tangy sauce underneath. There are many different formulas for making it and this one was sent to me by Pat Steggall of Marlborough in Wiltshire, who also supplied the recipe for Pear and Stilton Toasted Sandwich (see page 20).

EASY: *ready in an hour*

SERVES 4

50 g/2 oz butter
125 g/4 oz caster sugar
grated zest and juice of 1 lemon
2 medium or large eggs, separated

50 g/2 oz self-raising flour
300 ml/½ pint milk
double cream, to serve (optional)

❶ Beat the butter and sugar with the lemon zest until pale and fluffy. Add the yolks and flour, beat well and then gradually stir in the milk and a tbsp of lemon juice. The mixture may look a bit lumpy but this is correct.

❷ Whisk the egg whites till peaks form and fold in. Pour into a buttered 600 ml/1-pint dish and stand in a pan of hot water to come about halfway up the sides of the dish. Cook at 200°C/180°C fan oven/Gas Mark 6 for 45 minutes. (I have cooked this without the roasting tin of water and it still works, but the sauce may seem a little grainier than it might be.) I like to serve this with extra cream.

T I P One modern invention that makes this pudding more of a pleasure to make than ever is the Microplane Grater, my favourite discovery of last year. It costs a bomb at about £16 (from kitchen shops or Lakeland) but makes grating practically effortless.

SUMMER BERRY GRATIN

If you are lucky enough to live near a pick-your-own farm, this recipe is made for you. It is a joyous tumble of whatever soft fruit you can lay your hands on – the more different varieties the better – and it is the sort of dish that is ideal if you have invited a crowd to lunch, as it is easily multiplied up.

VERY EASY: *allow 35 minutes*

SERVES 6

For the fruit:

625 g/1¼ lb mixed raspberries, blueberries, blackberries and strawberries (hulled and sliced if large)

1 tbsp sugar

1 tbsp kirsch or other eau de vie (see Tip)

For the topping:

3 slices of white bread, crusts on

25 g/1 oz butter

50 g/2 oz light or dark brown sugar – muscovado has the finest flavour

a pinch of ground cinnamon

❶ Preheat the oven to 200°C/180°C fan oven/Gas Mark 6. Toss the fruit gently with the sugar and liqueur and a pinch of salt and transfer to a 23 cm/9-inch ovenproof dish.

❷ Pulse the topping ingredients in a food processor until it looks like coarse crumbs. Sprinkle over the fruit and bake for about 15–20 minutes. Leave for 5 minutes to cool a little and serve – with cream or crème fraîche if you wish.

T I P 🥄 I have long added kirsch – cherry eau-de-vie – to desserts to give them a subtle lift, but now I have discovered the most wonderful British eau-de-vie made from apples by the Somerset Cider Brandy Company. If you are a fan of really elegant cider (as fine as any wine), brandy (as fine as any Calvados) and other distinctive and not-too-sweet natural apple drinks, you need to know about this company, which can be contacted on 01460 420782.

CHOCOLATE CREAM PIE

Well worth making when you want to impress.

WORTH THE TROUBLE: *allow a morning*

SERVES 8–10

For the crust:

16 chocolate digestive biscuits

**40 g/1½ oz unsalted butter, melted
    and cooled**

For the filling:

600 ml/1 pint double cream

a pinch of salt

75 g/3 oz golden caster sugar

2 tbsp cornflour

6 large egg yolks

50 g/2 oz unsalted butter

**200 g/7 oz best-quality dark
    chocolate, chopped finely**

1 tsp vanilla extract

For the topping:

350 ml/12 fl oz whipping cream

1½ tbsp sugar

½ tsp vanilla extract

❶ To make the crust: process the biscuits till crumbly and mix with the butter. Use to line the bottom and up the sides of a 23 cm/9-inch pie dish or tin. Refrigerate for 20 minutes. Meanwhile, preheat the oven to 180°C/160°C fan oven/Gas Mark 4, then bake the crust for 15 minutes, till set.

❷ To make the filling: bring the cream, salt and 3 tbsp of the sugar to a simmer, stirring. Stir the remaining sugar and cornflour together in a small bowl, sprinkle over the egg yolks and whisk until the sugar has dissolved – about a minute.

❸ Pour a little of the hot cream mixture into the yolks and stir, then whisk that mixture back into the cream. Simmer until it thickens slightly – this should happen in less than half a minute.

❹ Off the heat, whisk in the butter and then the chocolate, until melted. Stir in the vanilla and pour into the cooled crust. Refrigerate for at least 3 hours.

❺ To make the topping: whip the cream and then whisk in the sugar and vanilla till smooth and thick and spread over the filling. Serve within an hour.

MAPLE SYRUP ICE CREAM

Maple syrup is one of the most fascinating of 'crops'. In March, medium and large sugar maples all over New England and Canada have a small tap drilled into their trunks. When the sap starts to rise – and a mature tree can produce several gallons overnight – buckets or pipes are connected to the taps and the sap collected; the amount collected can be spectacular when warm days are followed by frosty nights.

The great American inventor and president (of Pennsylvania) Benjamin Franklin had a dream that the United States would be self-sufficient in sugar, and make all its own from maple sap. The labour intensiveness of the system meant all hope was abandoned after a few years, but making maple syrup is still a favourite hobby of New Englanders in late spring, and no April Sunday would be complete without a syrup breakfast (waffles, French toast) in a sugar shack!

NO COOKING: *allow 30–40 minutes with an electric ice cream maker, or make a day ahead*

SERVES 6 – 8

500 g carton of bought fresh custard

1.2 litres/2 pints whipping cream
250 ml/8 fl oz maple syrup

❶ Beat the ingredients well in a large bowl.

❷ Chill in the fridge, then either freeze in an ice cream maker according to machine instructions, or put in a metal bowl and beat every hour till frozen. Serve with extra maple syrup poured over.

> **T I P** 🥣 You can add toasted chopped nuts to the mixture if you wish.

RHUBARB FOOL

Here I present a recipe that makes the most of that pretty and economical fruit, rhubarb, (though it is in fact technically a vegetable), sent in by a Daily Express *reader. As my correspondent points out, it is a fool with a difference, in that you end up with a striped dessert, rather like a knickerbocker glory.*

EASY: *allow 45 minutes, cook rhubarb in advance*

SERVES 8: EASILY HALVED

1.05 kg/2¼ lb rhubarb, trimmed   **a pinch of salt**

juice of 1 large orange   **450 ml/¾ pint double cream**

250 g/8 oz golden caster sugar

❶ To remove excess acidity, soak the rhubarb in cold water for 20 minutes. Drain, pat dry and cut in 1 cm/½-inch slices.

❷ Bring the orange juice, 175 g/6 oz of the sugar and the salt to the boil in a pan over a medium to high heat. Add the rhubarb and bring back to the boil, then reduce the heat and simmer for 7–10 minutes. Don't stir more than twice or three times or you will turn the pieces to mush. Cool to room temperature, then chill (an hour, or up to 24 hours).

❸ Whip the cream and remaining sugar till just thick.

❹ To assemble, take tall glasses and spoon about 50 ml/2 fl oz of rhubarb into each, then cream, then rhubarb, finishing with cream. Cover with plastic wrap and refrigerate for up to 6 hours. Alternatively, you can arrange the dessert in a large glass bowl to make just one fool.

TIP 🥣 An important point, when layering up the rhubarb, is not to use too much juice, as it will spoil the effect and make the fool wet.

chapter 8

BEAUTIFUL BAKES

There is something supremely satisfying about baking a cake or cookie. The miracle of mixing together ingredients, then seeing them rise into something wholesome, beautiful to behold and luscious to eat never ceases to amaze me.

In this chapter you'll find a selection of my favourites, including no less than three chocolate cakes, as I believe there's always room for another chocolate cake in your repertoire (and one is even low in fat!). Many of these bakes have a story behind them, which only adds to the charm when they come out of the oven in all their billowy wonderment.

MARGARET'S CARAMEL NUT SQUARES

I gleaned this recipe from a drinks party at Winfield House, the American Ambassador's residence in Regent's Park, London. It was developed by Margaret Fineran, the pastry chef, one of a brigade of four headed up by head chef Philip Dyer, who provide all the food for the Ambassador's entertaining (try 400 for drinks, or 100 for dinner) and family needs.

Margaret was born in Providence, Rhode Island, and worked at the White House for 3 years. Which leads me to a fascinating White House custom: at a drinks party savoury canapés are served and, to signal the close of the party, a round of sweet canapés – dessert in miniature, as it were – is sent out. I have no doubt that ex-President Clinton and Hillary loved tucking in to a tray of this hyper-nutty confection before retiring to their own apartment at the White House, kicking off their shoes and slobbing out in front of the television.

WORTH THE TROUBLE: *allow 45 minutes to make, 20 minutes to bake*

MAKES 9 SQUARES TO SERVE AS DESSERT, OR CUT SMALLER FOR PETITS FOURS

For the pastry:

175 g/6 oz plain flour

50 g/2 oz icing sugar

75 g/3 oz cold butter, cut in cubes

½ tsp vanilla extract or seeds of one vanilla pod

1 small egg, beaten

For the fruit and nuts:

125 g/4 oz pecan nuts

125 g/4 oz flaked almonds

125 g/4 oz whole hazelnuts

125 g/4 oz pistachios

50 g/2 oz dried cranberries

For the caramel:

75 g/3 oz granulated sugar

175 g/6 oz clear honey

50 g/2 oz butter

284 ml carton of double cream

whipped cream, to serve

1 Preheat the oven to 180°C/fan oven 160°C/Gas Mark 4. Put the flour, icing sugar and butter in a food processor and whizz until it resembles breadcrumbs. Add the vanilla and beaten egg and pulse until the pastry comes together. Wrap in cling film and chill for 30 minutes.

2 Toast the nuts lightly until just faintly browned, but not golden. Set aside. Roll the pastry out on a lightly floured surface and use to line a 22–23 cm/8½–9-inch square fluted flan tin, or a 23 cm/9-inch round tin (in which case you will need to serve in slim wedges). Bake blind, without the usual greaseproof paper and baking beans, for 7 minutes until just beginning to colour very faintly, but not golden.

3 Meanwhile, make the caramel. Put the sugar and honey in a small pan over a medium heat and bring to the boil without stirring. Melt the butter with the cream in the microwave for 2 minutes or in a separate pan until the cream is hot. When the sugar and honey mixture is boiling and looks frothy, pour in the hot cream and butter and simmer, stirring, for 2–3 minutes.

4 Tip the nuts and cranberries into the caramel and mix well. Spoon into the hot pastry case, pouring over any leftover caramel. Return to the oven for 7 minutes.

5 Remove from the oven, cool completely in the tin, cover and freeze for 3–4 hours. When frozen, cut in squares in the tin and leave the squares to thaw on a plate for 30 minutes. Serve with softly whipped cream.

T I P 🥣 Freezing the mixture for 3–4 hours sets the nuts in the caramel and makes cutting the squares much easier.

CHOCOLATE CHIP THINS

*These are not your thick, soft, chunky American-style chocolate chip
cookies, but thin crisp ones, which snap with a wonderful buttery crunch.
They keep well in a tin or jar for a week – if you can resist them.*

WORTH THE TROUBLE: *allow 40 minutes*

MAKES 3–4 DOZEN BISCUITS

210 g/7½ oz plain flour

a good pinch of salt

¾ tsp bicarbonate of soda

125 g/4 oz butter, melted and cooled

125 g/4 oz granulated sugar

65 g/2½ oz light brown or light
   muscovado sugar

3 tbsp golden syrup

1 large egg yolk

2 tbsp milk

1 tbsp vanilla extract

140 g/4½ oz chocolate chips or
   chopped plain chocolate

1 Line two trays with baking parchment. Preheat the oven to 190°C/180°C
fan oven/Gas Mark 5. Put the flour, salt and bicarb into a bowl and set aside.

2 In a mixer, beat the butter, sugars and syrup for a minute, then add
the egg yolk, milk and vanilla. Now add the flour mixture and mix till
combined (do not overwork); then add the chocolate.

3 Roll tablespoon-sized balls of the mixture and space out generously
on the baking sheets with at least 3 cm/1 inch distance all the way
around them. Bake until golden and flat, about 10–12 minutes.

4 Cool the biscuits on the tin for 3 minutes, then lift on to wire rack.
Repeat with the remaining mixture.

TIP 🥄 As with many biscuit recipes, you can make the dough
up to 2 days ahead and keep in the fridge or freeze it for longer.
Bring to room temperature before shaping and baking.

DOUBLE CHOCOLATE
BROWNIES

*Here is a rich, glossy brownie that presents no problems in the making
and keeps beautifully in the fridge.*

FUN TO MAKE: *allow a good hour*

CUTS INTO 12–16 BROWNIES

200 g/7 oz dark chocolate	300 g/10 oz caster sugar
125 g/4 oz butter, diced roughly	2 tsp vanilla extract
3 tbsp cocoa powder	½ tsp salt
3 large eggs	130 g/4½ oz plain flour

❶ Preheat the oven to 180°C/160°C fan oven/Gas Mark 4. Grease a
20 cm/8-inch square baking tray. Line the tray with foil, allowing a good
overhang on all sides (which you will be using to lift out the brownies
later). Grease the foil.

❷ Melt the chocolate and butter (easiest in a microwave). Whisk in the
cocoa till smooth and set aside.

❸ Whisk together the eggs, sugar, vanilla and salt till combined – about
15 seconds. Whisk the warm chocolate mixture in, then stir in the flour
with a wooden spoon till just combined. Pour into the pan, spread into
corners and level surface with a rubber spatula.

❹ Bake for about 35–40 minutes, till the cake is slightly puffed and a
toothpick inserted in the centre comes out with just a few sticky crumbs
attached. Cool to room temperature in the tin, then lift out using the foil
and cut in rectangles or squares.

T I P S Do not overmix at step 3. The flour needs to be just
combined.

Do not overcook in step 4. Brownies are meant to be soft and
fudgy in the centre.

Best stored as a whole cake, then squares cut off just before eating
if this is practical. They will keep refrigerated for up to 5 days.

EMILY'S GINGERBREAD

Here is a recipe with a story behind it. It concerns the American poet Emily Dickinson, who lived in Amherst (pronounced 'amerst' – the h is silent) in New England in the mid nineteenth century. Everything we know about Emily is rather strange and fascinating and over the years she has turned into a cult poet. Her minimalistic poetry – short, epigrammatic, full of domestic and household imagery – was almost exclusively written in her small bedroom in the family house to the north of the town, and in her late 20s and 30s she seems to have turned into something of a recluse, rarely leaving the house or seeing visitors.

From letters and diaries we know that Emily hated cleaning, but she loved cooking – her hard-to-please father called her bread the best he ever tasted. Cooking in those days was no doddle – you had to get a good fire going, put the coals in the oven and remove them at just the right time. You had to measure dry ingredients from barrels and there was nothing pre-prepared. (While waiting for the oven to heat she would often jot a line of a poem down on a flour bag or whatever.) Emily left us her recipe for gingerbread, which was a huge favourite with her niece and nephews and the local children. Because of her increasing shyness, she would lower the gingerbread down via a knotted rope from her bedroom window in a little straw basket with a lid.

MAKE THIS IN HONOUR OF EMILY: *allow 45 minutes*

MAKES 12 LARGE GINGERBREADS –
EAT QUICKLY AS IT DOESN'T IMPROVE
WITH KEEPING

50 g/2 oz butter, softened

50 ml/2 fl oz double or whipping
  cream

125 ml/4 fl oz golden syrup,
  molasses or treacle

275 g/9 oz plain flour

1½ tsp ground ginger

½ tsp bicarbonate of soda

½ tsp salt

granulated sugar or beaten egg,
  to glaze

1 Preheat the oven to 180°C/160°C fan oven/Gas Mark 4. Grease one large or two small baking sheets.

2 Cream the butter, cream and syrup. Stir in the flour, ginger, bicarb and salt. Spoon out heaped tbsp of the mixture and shape into flattened ovals about 7.5 cm/3 inches long – the dough is sticky – and put on the baking sheet(s).

3 Emily used to vary the glaze. Either brush the tops with water (or moisten with wet fingers) then sprinkle with sugar, or brush with beaten egg. Bake for 20 minutes, till just firm. Cool on a wire rack. Emily would decorate with pansies or other small edible flowers from the garden or her conservatory.

GINGER SPONGE CAKE, WITH GINGER ICING

This is a perfect bake from the New White Horse Cookbook. *The charity cookbook in question was first published in 1995, recently reprinted, and you can get your copy by sending a cheque for £7.50 (£6 plus £1.50 post and packing), made payable to St Mary's Church, to Mrs Fenella Oberman, Norton House, Uffington, Oxfordshire SN7 7RA. This easy and attractive ginger cake was donated by Helen Gantlett, who mentions that it is the cake that graces the Uffington Summer Tea, a famous local event.*

EASY: *ready in a couple of hours, including 1–1¹/₄ hours baking; freezes well*

CUTS INTO 8

175 g/6 oz butter, softened

175 g/6 oz soft brown sugar or caster sugar (or a mixture of both)

3 large eggs

175 g/6 oz self-raising flour, sifted with 2 tsp ground ginger

2 tbsp milk

For the icing:

75 g/3 oz softened butter

75 g/3 oz icing sugar, sifted

1 tsp ground ginger

1 tsp golden syrup

❶ Preheat the oven to 180°C/160°C fan oven/Gas Mark 4. Grease and line a 20 cm/8-inch round tin or a 19 cm/7½-inch square tin. Put all ingredients in a mixing bowl and beat for a minute with a wooden spoon. Turn into the tin and hollow the centre slightly.

❷ Bake for about an hour and a quarter to an hour and a half. Turn out on to a wire rack to cool.

❸ To make the icing: put all ingredients in a small saucepan and heat gently. When smooth, remove from heat, allow to cool and when thick pour over the cake.

IRENE HANDL'S VIENNESE
CHOCOLATE CAKE

Vivienne Coombe of Bosham, Chichester wrote to me with this simple and exceptional recipe from Irene Handl. 'I have made it every year for 30 years – "rich but light" was Irene Handl's description and that is spot on!'

WORTH THE TROUBLE: *allow 1¹/2 hours, including ³/4–1 hour baking; freezes well or keeps well wrapped in cling film or foil*

CUTS INTO 8

For the cake:

125 g/4 oz unsalted butter

125 g/4 oz caster sugar

grated zest of 1 orange

grated zest of 1 lemon

a small pinch of ground cinnamon

a small pinch of ground cloves

1 tsp almond essence

50 g/2 oz plain chocolate, melted

125 g/4 oz ground almonds

2 large eggs, beaten

2 tsp rum or brandy

50 g/2 oz self-raising flour

For the icing:

3 tbsp orange marmalade

1 tbsp rum or brandy

125 g/4 oz plain chocolate, melted

a small knob of butter

chocolate leaves, to decorate

(optional)

❶ Grease and bottom-line a 23 × 13 cm/9 × 5 inch loaf tin. Preheat the oven to 180°C/160°C fan oven/Gas Mark 4. Cream the butter and sugar with the zest, spices and essence. Add the chocolate and ground almonds and beat well. Add the eggs, rum or brandy and flour gradually. Turn the mixture into the tin, smooth the top and bake for ³/4–1 hour, till firm to the touch. Cool on a wire rack.

❷ To finish, brush the cake all over with the marmalade, which you have warmed and thinned with the rum or brandy. Beat the butter into the chocolate and, while still warm and glossy, spread all over the marmaladed cake. Decorate with chocolate leaves if you wish. Serve in slices, with whipped cream if serving as dessert.

ITALIAN FRUIT CAKE

This recipe was sent in by Daily Express *reader Francesco Manzoli.
'I would like to send you a recipe for a cake that has been in the family
for many years. My uncle and father worked at the Savoy Hotel in
1912. It was my uncle who was given the recipe by the pastry cook
and took it back to Italy in 1920, where he opened a hotel in Baveno
on Lago Maggiore called the Hotel Suisse and served it to the
predominantly English clientele.' Mr Manzoli brought the recipe
back to Britain and served it in his Knightsbridge restaurant called
La Speranza, which he closed in 1970. The extraordinary thing is
that when Mr Manzoli later returned to Baveno, this cake had
become the speciality of the town!*

STRAIGHTFORWARD: *allow 2 hours, including 1¹/4–1¹/2 hours baking*

CUTS INTO 6–8

175 g/6 oz unsalted butter, softened   1 tsp baking powder

175 g/6 oz caster sugar   175 g/6 oz mixed dried fruit

3 medium eggs   1 tsp vanilla extract

175 g/6 oz plain flour – Italian 00
  flour if you can get it

❶ Preheat the oven to 180°C/160°C fan oven/Gas Mark 4. Butter and
line an 18–19 cm/7–7¹/2-inch cake tin. Using an electric hand whisk, mix
the butter and sugar till creamy, add the eggs and the flour sifted with
the baking powder – beating after each addition – then fold in the fruit
and vanilla. (Mr Manzoli mixes this all in one step using a heavy hand
whisk, but the first time you make it, be sure everything is perfectly
mixed by doing as above.)

❷ Bake for an hour, then turn the oven down by 10°C and cook for a
further 15–30 minutes, testing with a skewer before removing from oven.

LEMON FEATHER CAKE

This cake is made with potato flour. Not only does this make it very light, but it means coeliacs and others with a wheat intolerance can enjoy it. You can find potato flour in delicatessens and health food shops. The other investment for this recipe you might wish to make, if you haven't one already, is a moule manqué *tin. This is a large shallow tin with sloping sides.*

NO PROBLEM: *20 minutes to make, 35–45 minutes to bake; freezes well at end of step 2, or when assembled (dust with icing sugar later)*

CUTS INTO 10

6 large eggs, separated
300 g/10 oz caster sugar
grated zest and juice of 1 lemon
160 g/5½ oz potato flour

For the filling:
284 ml carton of double or
   whipping cream
225 ml/7 fl oz lemon curd or 100 ml/
   3½ fl oz lemon liqueur (limoncello)
icing sugar, for dusting

❶ Preheat the oven to 180°C/160°C fan oven/Gas Mark 4. Butter a 25 cm/ 10-inch *moule manqué* tin and line the base with buttered paper. Dust all with caster sugar, then with potato flour. Whisk the yolks with the sugar, zest and juice with an electric mixer for 3–5 minutes till thick and mousse-like. Fold in the potato flour till smooth.

❷ Whisk the egg whites in a clean bowl till stiff and fold into the other mixture. Turn into the tin and bake for 35 minutes, till just firm. The cake will sink slightly. Turn out after 5 minutes and cool on a rack.

❸ When cold, split and fill with the filling. Make this by folding beaten lemon curd into the lightly whipped cream, or whipping the cream and adding the liqueur when semi-stiff, then whipping together till stiff. Dust with icing sugar and serve.

LEMON PINE KERNEL TART

This exceptional dessert is the invention of Italian cook Susanna Gelmetti.

SPECIAL AND DELICIOUS: *30 minutes to prepare, 45 minutes to cook*

CUTS INTO 8

For the pastry:

250 g/8 oz plain flour

125 g/4 oz butter

75 g/3 oz caster sugar

2 large egg yolks

grated zest of 1 lemon

For the filling:

4 medium egg yolks

150 g/5 oz caster sugar

40 g/1½ oz plain flour

300 ml/½ pint milk

200 ml//7 fl oz cream

grated zest of 1 lemon

150 g/5 oz pine kernels

icing sugar, to dust

mascarpone or double cream, to serve

❶ Make the pastry by putting the flour and butter in a processor and whizzing, then adding the sugar, egg yolks and zest. The mixture will almost come together to form a ball. Turn into a deep 23–26 cm/9–10-inch flan tin (it must be at least 3 cm/1½ inches deep or you will have too much filling) and, using two forks or your fingers, as you prefer, press out and up the sides to form a neat pastry case with no gaps. Refrigerate while you make the filling, and preheat the oven to 190°C/170°C fan oven/ Gas Mark 5.

❷ Beat the egg yolks with the sugar till thick and whisk in the flour, then the milk, cream and lemon. Tranfer to a pan and cook till thickened like custard – should take less than 5 minutes. Stir all the time but do not be overly concerned as the flour will prevent the custard from curdling.

❸ Pour the filling into the chilled pastry case – do not overfill or it will expand and overflow. Sprinkle all over thickly with the pine kernels and bake for 45 minutes, till well browned (though it will still feel a little wobbly). Allow to cool and serve warm or cool.

❹ Dust with icing sugar to serve; lovely with mascarpone or double cream.

LOAF OF GOODNESS

This delectable fruit loaf is jam-packed with healthy ingredients.
EASY: *start a day ahead; freezes well*

CUTS INTO 10

For the fruit:

**50 g/2 oz mi-cuit plums or prunes,
chopped roughly (see Tip)**

**50 g/2 oz organic dried apricots,
chopped roughly**

250 g/8 oz raisins or other dried fruit

150 g/5 oz muscovado sugar

300 ml/½ pint strong tea

For the loaf:

125 g/4 oz plain flour

2 tsp baking powder

1 tsp ground allspice

125 g/4 oz wholemeal flour

50 g/2 oz rolled oats or bran cereal

**50 g/2 oz butter or margarine
(optional)**

**75 g/3 oz mixed nuts and seeds,
chopped if large**

2 large eggs

**125 g/4 oz runny honey, plus extra
to glaze**

❶ Put the fruit and sugar in a bowl, cover with tea, pressing down if necessary and leave for 1 hour or overnight.

❷ Grease and base-line a 1.75-litre/3-pint loaf tin. Preheat the oven to 180°C/160°C fan oven/Gas Mark 4. Sift the plain flour, baking powder and spice and add the wholemeal flour and oats. Rub in the butter or margarine, if using. Stir in the soaked fruits and their liquid, nuts, eggs and honey and mix till evenly combined – the mixture is quite sloppy.

❸ Turn into the tin, level and bake for 1–1¼ hours, or until firm to the touch and a skewer inserted in centre comes out clean. Check after 45 minutes and cover with foil or a butter paper if it starts to get too brown, but do test carefully as it may look done before the centre is fully cooked.

❹ Drizzle with a little extra honey and leave to cool in the tin.

> **T I P** 🥄 Mi-cuit plums are soft semi-dried plums and are available vacuum-packed from the Merchant Gourmet range. If you can't find them, use soft, plump prunes instead.

MRS FYJIS-WALKER'S CHOCOLATE CAKE

I was introduced to this beautiful cake by my friend Gabriele, who knows it as 'Evi's Chocolate Cake'. It is flour-free – therefore suitable for coeliacs.

SIMPLE AND ELEGANT: *30 minutes to prepare, 50 minutes to bake; freezes well before icing and keeps very well indeed*

CUTS INTO 10

150 g/5 oz butter, at room
  temperature
6 large eggs, separated
150 g/5 oz caster sugar
150 g/5 oz ground almonds
150 g/5 oz best-quality plain
  chocolate, melted

For the icing:
3–4 tbsp apricot or other jam,
  warmed
150 g/5 oz plain chocolate, melted
2 tbsp very strong coffee
50 g/2 oz caster sugar
40 g/1½ oz buttter

❶ To make the cake, preheat the oven to 170°C/150°C fan oven/Gas Mark 4. Grease a 20 cm/8-inch springform tin thoroughly. Cream the butter and egg yolks thoroughly – don't worry if it looks a bit like scrambled egg at this point. Mix in the sugar, ground almonds and melted chocolate (cooled): the mixture will be very thick and heavy. Whisk the egg whites till stiff. Mix in a quarter of the egg whites, to slacken the mixture, then fold in the rest. Be patient as the mixture is still quite stiff and it takes a couple of minutes to get the two mixtures amalgamated. Transfer to the tin and bake for 50 minutes, till just firm and risen. Leave in tin for 5 minutes, then run a knife round the sides, unclip and transfer to a rack. The cake may dome in the middle – but don't worry, it will more or less sink back into place as it cools.

② When cool, remove the cake from the base of the tin and put on a serving plate. Spread with the top with the jam. Melt the chocolate in a small pan, stir in the coffee, sugar and butter and stir together over a low heat till smooth. The icing will be quite liquid and retain the crunch of some of the sugar – this is correct. Pour about half over the top of the cake and spread down over the sides with a small knife, adding a little more of the icing at the top of the sides and letting it trickle down as necessary. Any icing left after the sides are covered should be scooped with a spatula on to the top. The icing is lovely and shiny. Clean up the serving plate with damp kitchen paper. No further decoration is required.

T I P S This is a bit like the Austrian Sachertorte, a shiny confection which was at the centre of a long lawsuit regarding its authenticity.

You can vary the jam as you wish. Raspberry jam also goes well with chocolate, as does redcurrant jelly. If using jam with a lot of texture, warm then sieve it or it will make the top of the cake lumpy.

REFRIGERATOR COOKIES

These cookies are not made in the refrigerator or served chilled: but to make it easy to handle, the dough is refrigerated before baking. This is an American invention. The other secret of this recipe lies in the lemon oil. I came across the Boyajian range of oils on a visit to Boston, where they are produced, and was transfixed by the possibilities of the huge range. You can find a selection of the brightly coloured range from the brilliant Lakeland catalogue (call 015394 88100) or Sainsbury's Special Selection. If you can't find them, use 2 tsp finely grated lemon zest instead.

EASY AND FUN: *allow 35 minutes plus 4 hours chilling; dough keeps for a week before baking or freezes well*

MAKES UP TO 4 DOZEN BISCUITS

250 g/8 oz butter, softened	**1 tsp vanilla extract**
175 g/6 oz icing sugar, sifted	**2 tsp lemon oil**
2 large egg yolks	**250 g/8 oz plain flour**

❶ Cream the butter and sugar till light and fluffy, beat in the egg yolks one at a time and then the vanilla and lemon oil. Add the flour and beat till well blended.

❷ Divide the dough into three equal parts and form into sausages. Wrap in waxed paper or plastic film and refrigerate for at least 4 hours, till firm.

❸ When ready to bake, preheat the oven to 190°C/170°C fan oven/Gas Mark 5. Cut off thin slices of dough with your sharpest knife and lay on baking parchment on a baking sheet. Bake for 10–12 minutes; allow to cool slightly on the sheet before transferring to a rack.

STILTON BREAD

I spent a summer trying different bread recipes and, during my experiments, came across the most wonderful range of flours from Shipton Mill.

The flours are available from some delicatessens but you can call and collect or there is a brilliant mail-order service. For a list of dozens of different sorts of flour to experiment with, from the most beautiful organic plain flour I have ever touched to wondrous mixes with seeds and grains, drop them a line at Long Newnton, Tetbury, Gloucestershire GL8 8RP, telephone 01666 505050.

A PLEASURE TO MAKE: *made in a morning or afternoon; freezes well*

MAKES 2 SMALL LOAVES

625 g/1½ lb strong plain flour	100 g/4 oz Stilton, plus a little
125 g/4 oz strong plain wholemeal	extra
flour	½ tsp fast-action dried yeast
1 tbsp salt	450 ml/½ pint warm water

❶ Process the flours, salt and half the Stilton. Add the yeast and then the warm water and mix to a dough. Knead for 10 minutes, or 5 minutes in a mixer, till supple and no longer sticky. Set aside for 1½–2 hours, till doubled in bulk.

❷ Grease two 500 g/1 lb loaf tins or the equivalent. Knock the dough down and knead in the rest of the Stilton, chopped small. Shape and place in tins. Allow to rise for 30 minutes. Preheat the oven to 230°C/210°C fan oven/Gas Mark 8, crumble a little extra Stilton over the top and bake for about 15 minutes. Then reduce the heat to 200°C/180°C fan oven/ Gas Mark 6 and bake for a further 15–20 minutes, till cooked.

T I P In this recipe the Stilton provides both the necessary fat and the flavour, so no oil or butter is required

---

SURREY APPLE CAKE

This quick and easy cake makes good use of the apple harvest and was sent to me at the Daily Express *by Mrs Couzens of Lower Bourne, Farnham.*

EASY: *30 minutes to prepare, 1 hour in the oven*

ENOUGH FOR 8 SERVINGS

For the cake mixture:

150 g/5 oz softened butter

75 g/3 oz caster sugar

1 medium egg

250 g/8 oz self-raising flour

For the filling:

500 g/1 lb cooking apples, peeled, cored and sliced

3 tbsp apricot jam

2 tbsp demerara or other soft brown sugar

double cream, to serve

❶ Preheat the oven to 160°C/140°C fan oven/Gas Mark 3. Butter a 20 cm/8-inch springform cake tin. Put the cake ingredients in a mixer and beat till smooth and sticky; then press two-thirds of the mixture into the base of the tin, using your fingers.

❷ Top with the apples, then dot over the jam and sprinkle with sugar. Put the remaining cake mixture in blobs to roughly cover the top, then bake for an hour. Serve cold or warm with cream.

> **T I P** 🥣 If you wish, you can sprinkle this with flaked almonds or demerara sugar before baking.

BANANA CAKE WITH
COCONUT CREAM

*I discovered this recipe on a visit to Liverpool. The city is spotless
and beautiful once more, and it deserves its new prosperity. I gleaned
this cake recipe from Billingtons, the sugar company based in Liverpool,
and it is such a winner that I made it for a birthday celebration.*
EASY: *allow 1³/4 hours; cake can be frozen before icing*

CUTS INTO 10

For the cake:

5 large ripe bananas

150 g/5 oz butter, softened

350 g/11 oz self-raising flour

¹/2 tsp bicarbonate of soda

250 g/8 oz light muscovado sugar

3 large eggs

150 g/5 oz pecans or walnuts

sweetened coconut shreds,
  optional, to decorate

For the coconut cream (optional):

50 g/2 oz block of creamed coconut

3 tbsp hot water

425 ml/14 fl oz double cream

2 tbsp golden icing sugar, plus
  extra to decorate

❶ Preheat the oven to 180°C/160°C fan oven/Gas Mark 4. Grease and
line a 20 cm/8-inch loose-bottomed tin.

❷ Make the coconut cream first. Process the coconut and water until
smooth, then add the cream and icing sugar. Process with the pulse
button till lightly whipped, transfer to a bowl and chill.

❸ There is no need to wash up the processor bowl. Add the bananas
and process till mashed. Add all remaining cake ingredients except the
nuts and process until well mixed. Then add the nuts and pulse until
they are just chopped roughly.

❹ Turn into the tin and level the surface. Bake for 1–1¹/2 hours, till a
skewer inserted into the centre of the cake comes out clean. Allow to
cool, then peel off the lining paper.

❺ Before serving, spoon the coconut cream over the top and sides of
the cake. If you wish, finish with coconut shreds and more icing sugar.

CHOCOLATE AND
WALNUT CAKE

This is a low-fat cake – one of those extremely clever recipes in which dates are used to take the place of quantities of butter. It is healthy in other ways too, containing ground walnuts (which contain omega-3 fatty acids) and golden caster sugar.

In my kitchen I always make a point of using unrefined sugars. So here are my three golden rules when choosing sugar: firstly, always make sure it has 'unrefined' on the label. If it doesn't say unrefined that's because it's almost certainly refined. Secondly, if a recipe specifies soft light brown or soft dark brown sugar, I always use light or dark muscovado instead. If it says demerara, use demerara – but make sure you buy demerara. It may sound hilarious, but many refined demerara sugars are simply white sugar sprayed brown! What are the benefits? Unrefined sugar is a fully natural product, it is fairly traded (though because most of it doesn't come from the poorest countries, it can't technically be called Fairtrade) and the flavour is incomparable.

FUN TO MAKE: *allow 2 hours, including 25 minutes baking; freezes well*

CUTS INTO 10

For the cake:

75 g/3 oz chopped pitted dates

25 g/1 oz unsweetened cocoa powder

125 ml/4 fl oz boiling water

1 tsp instant coffee granules

25 g/1 oz slice of fresh white bread

50 g/2 oz walnut halves, toasted in the oven

40 g/1½ oz plain flour

¼ tsp salt

140 g/2 oz golden caster sugar

2 tbsp sunflower oil

1 tsp vanilla extract

1 large egg, plus 3 large egg whites

For the glaze:

25 g/1 oz unsweetened cocoa powder

40 g/1½ oz plain chocolate, chopped finely

50 ml/2 fl oz boiling water

1 tbsp golden syrup

1 tsp instant coffee granules

½ tsp vanilla extract

125 g/4 oz golden icing sugar

❶ Preheat the oven to 180°C/160°C fan oven/Gas Mark 4. Grease a 23 cm/9-inch cake tin and base-line with baking parchment.

❷ Combine the dates, cocoa, boiling water and coffee and let stand for 20 minutes. Process the bread to form coarse crumbs and put in a medium bowl. Reserve 10 toasted walnut pieces for garnish and process the remaining walnuts, with the flour and salt, till finely ground. Remove and add to the bowl containing the breadcrumbs. No need to wash up the processor but put in the date mixture with half the caster sugar, oil, vanilla and whole egg and process till smooth. Now mix the wet and dry mixes together till just smooth.

❸ Whisk the egg whites till soft peaks form, then add the remaining caster sugar, 1 tbsp at a time, till stiff and glossy. Fold a quarter into the cake batter to loosen, then the rest. Spread into tin and bake for 25 minutes or until slightly springy to the touch. Cool for 10 minutes in the tin and then on a rack.

❹ To make the glaze, combine the cocoa, chocolate, water, syrup and coffee and stir till smooth. Stir in the vanilla and then cover and chill for an hour. Gradually add the icing sugar to this mixture, using an electric beater if you have one, till thick. Spread the glaze on the cake and top with the 10 reserved walnut pieces.

GOLDEN CORNBREAD

*Some of those reading may have memories stretching back to 1992,
which was the year I first started cooking seriously, thanks to my
appearance (as a contestant!) on the Masterchef programme. One of
the dishes I made on the show was cornbread, though I was never
quite happy with the recipe. One of the many advantages of getting
older (in this particular case, nine years older) is that you have time to
perfect the mistakes of your youth, so here is a much better recipe than
Loyd Grossman (who then presented the programme) was given to
taste by me.*

EASY: *allow 1 hour 10 minutes; freezes well*

CUTS INTO 8–10

275 g/9 oz cornmeal (or polenta)	**2 large eggs**
350 g/11 oz plain flour	**475 ml/16 fl oz milk**
125 g/4 oz golden caster sugar	**25 g/1 oz butter, melted, plus extra**
7 tsp baking powder	**for the pan**
¾ tsp salt	

❶ Preheat the oven to 180°C/160°C fan oven/Gas Mark 4. Lightly butter
a 20 cm/8-inch square baking tin and, if you wish, line the base with
baking parchment, as I do find cornbread has an inclination to stick.

❷ In a large bowl, mix the cornmeal, flour, sugar, baking powder and
salt. Set aside.

❸ Lightly beat the eggs, then add the milk and butter. Slowly stir this
mixture into the cornmeal and stop immediately it is incorporated.
Scrape this batter into the tin.

❹ Bake until light brown and a skewer inserted into the centre comes
out clean – about 45–55 minutes. Transfer to a wire rack to cool, then
cut in wedges. Serve warm, or as fresh as possible after baking, with
butter. Great for breakfast or with Mediterranean food.

LAVENDER SHORTBREAD

Lavender is one of the lesser known products of Western Massachusetts in the United States, where it grows with fragrant abandon during the rather short summer. My recipe comes the charming gift shop in Greenfield, Franklin County, Massachusetts.

Cooking with flowers is not to everyone's taste but, if you grow lavender, you will certainly enjoy this different bake. Harvest the lavender in midsummer, dry it, then snip the flowers finely and serve these biscuits with ice cream. Without the lavender, incidentally, this is simply a very fine shortbread recipe.

WORTH THE TROUBLE: *allow a morning, including 2 hours resting*

MAKES ABOUT 2 DOZEN BISCUITS

125 g/4 oz butter, softened

60 g/2½ oz golden caster sugar

1–2 tsp (no more) finely snipped
   lavender, dried

140 g/4½ oz plain flour

25 g/1 oz cornflour

a pinch of salt

icing sugar, for dusting (see Tip)

❶ Preheat the oven to 160°C/160°C also for fan oven/Gas Mark 3. In a bowl, cream the butter, sugar and lavender. Combine the flours and salt and beat into the creamed mix. Cover and refrigerate for 2 hours, until firm enough to handle. Roll out to 5 mm/¼ inch thickness on a floured surface and then cut in 4 cm/1½-inch squares.

❷ Put on to ungreased baking sheets, well spaced, prick with a fork several times and bake for 18–22 minutes or until the edges are lightly browned. Cool for a minute before removing to wire racks to cool completely. Sift over a little icing sugar and serve.

TIP 🥄 For home-made lavender icing sugar, mix 125 g/4 oz of icing sugar with ½ tsp lavender. Set aside at room temperature for 24 hours, sift and use.

SOUTHERN COMFORT CAKE

Southern Comfort in fact comes from deeper south than Kentucky. The recipe is a secret (invented by a clever bartender), and although it has a reputation for being a young person's tipple it is in fact a voluptuously fruity spirit that, once tasted, you will not forget. If you invest in a bottle – and I recommend it – you can make yourself a Scarlett O'Hara by mixing Southern Comfort, peach nectar (rather like mango nectar, in cartons) and cranberry juice. It is a warm pinky orange colour, and you pour it over lots of ice and sip with a sprig of mint. Or try this luscious cake.

DELICIOUSLY DIFFERENT: *allow a couple of hours, including 1¼–1½ hours baking; make a day ahead*

CUTS INTO 10–12

175 g/6 oz butter, at room
   temperature
375 g/12 oz golden caster sugar
6 large eggs
125 ml/4 fl oz Southern Comfort

1 tbsp grated orange zest
1 tbsp vanilla extract
250 g/8 oz plain flour
½ tsp salt

❶ Preheat the oven to 160°C/150°C fan oven/Gas Mark 3. Butter and flour a 20 cm/8-inch cake tin.

❷ Cream the butter in a large bowl, gradually add the sugar and beat until pale and fluffy. Beat in the eggs, one at a time, then the Southern Comfort, orange zest and vanilla.

❸ Beat in the flour and salt until blended, then pour the batter into the prepared tin.

❹ Bake until golden brown, about 1¼–1½ hours. Cool for 10 minutes, then turn out and finish cooling. Do not cut on the day of eating, but save for tomorrow and the day after. Wrap in foil and serve with tea or coffee.

chapter 9

NO COOKING REQUIRED!

One of the most fun sorts of cooking is not cooking at all, but mixing ingredients together to form something inventive and wonderful. Some clever people have this down to a fine art, and buy almost all the components of a party – just heating through the sauce and boiling the pasta for instance. If you actually enjoy cooking, this would cheat you of much of the pleasure of entertaining, but it is really convenient sometimes to have a starter and/or dessert in the bag before you even start to cook, and if it's an ingenious assembly of other ingredients so much the better.

There is only one rule with no-cook recipes: make sure every ingredient is the very best, as there is nothing to disguise it.

AVOCADO AND CHESHIRE CHEESE SALAD

This is a very elegant and easy starter; the only possible disadvantage is that there is a little last-minute preparation.

This recipe was devised by Winkfield, Surrey's famous cookery school until the 1980s, and they suggested that you serve the salad in stoned, halved avocados, instead of skinning the avocados and slicing as I prefer. If this is how you choose to serve it, the recipe will only serve four.

SIMPLE AND ELEGANT: *30 minutes to prepare, no cooking*

SERVES 4 – 6

2 ripe tomatoes	**2 ripe avocados**
75 g/3 oz Cheshire cheese	**1 tbsp chopped fresh herbs, such**
2 tsp tomato purée	**as basil and chives or mint and**
¼ tsp caster sugar	**parsley**
1 tbsp wine vinegar	**salt and pepper**
4 tbsp sunflower oil	**85 g bag of watercress, to serve**

❶ Pour boiling water over the tomatoes, and slip off the skins. Put a small sieve over a bowl. Cut the tomatoes in quarters and, over the sieve, squeeze out seeds and juice; press down on the seeds to get out all the juice. Put the tomato flesh on a board, chop and put in another bowl; crumble in the cheese and set aside.

❷ Make the dressing by whisking the tomato purée, sugar, vinegar, oil and plenty of pepper and salt into the tomato juice. Taste and add more seasoning if necessary.

❸ So far can be done in advance. Halve, stone, peel and roughly chop the avocados and fold into the tomato-cheese mixture, trying not to break up too much. At the last minute, arrange the watercress in nests on plates. Divide the cheese mixture between the watercress nests, whisk the herbs into the dressing and spoon over the salad. Serve at once.

DIME BAR ICE CREAM

This ice cream is something of a novelty, consisting of crushed confectionery stirred into ice cream. When I was experimenting with it I looked up a couple of other ice cream recipes and stumbled across something far more eccentric, however. Really Wild Pudding consists of a round of black pudding and a scoop of vanilla ice cream topped with oodles of butterscotch sauce. I have to admit I haven't tried it, but Sue Lawrence, who included it in her Wardie Parish Cookbook, *says 'this has to be tried to be believed. The combination – bizarrely – works! Just don't look at what is in your spoon as you eat!'*

NO COOKING: *take ice cream out of freezer 15 minutes ahead*

SERVES 4 – 6

750 ml/1¼ pints Swedish glace　　**four 28 g Dime Bars (see Tip)**
(or other good-quality vanilla
ice cream – see Tip)

❶ Remove the ice cream 15 minutes before eating, or longer if using another, firmer, ice cream, to allow to soften.

❷ Roughly chop the Dime Bars. Fold in with a metal spoon and either serve at once or return to the freezer to firm up before scooping.

TIPS 🥄 Dime Bars are smallish, nut brittle chocolate bars in red packets. You will find them in many sweetshops and at Ikea too.

Swedish glace is a remarkable non-dairy, lactose- and cholesterol-free ice widely available from supermarkets. Look out for it – it is good for you and tastes delicious.

GINGER LEMON CREAM DESSERT

'Help,' came the plea from Daily Express reader Helen Tompkins of Epsom in Surrey. 'My husband absolutely adores St Michael lemon desserts (from their fresh cream range) but always complains they are too small and need to be four times the size!'

Now not many stores would yield up such a delicious secret, but the nice people at Marks and Spencer generously told me how to make this dessert. Their version is a model of good cooking – just six ingredients – so it has been easy to adapt for the home cook.

VERY EASY: allow 15 minutes, make 4 hours ahead

SERVES 4 – 6

75 g/3 oz ginger biscuits (I especially like M&S all-butter ginger biscuits with stem ginger – of these, you will need 3)

2 tbsp white wine or sherry

284 ml carton of double or whipping cream

250 ml carton of crème fraîche

3 tbsp caster sugar

grated zest and juice of 1 lemon

1 tbsp water

❶ Roughly crumble the biscuits into either individual glasses or a 1.2-litre/2-pint shallow serving dish – glass looks pretty because you can see the different layers. Sprinkle with the wine or sherry.

❷ Whip the cream, crème fraîche and sugar together. As the mixture begins to thicken, whisk in half the lemon zest, the water and the lemon juice. Stop whipping when it is thick and floppy.

❸ Spoon over the biscuits. Make at least 4 hours ahead or can be made up to a day ahead. Just before serving, sprinkle with the reserved lemon zest.

> **TIP** 🥣 Don't add the lemon zest until just before serving or it will go brown.

GREEN STREET DIP

At a lot of trendy restaurants nowadays the bread arrives with a little saucer of olive oil for dipping – or olive oil with a little balsamic vinegar poured into a slick in the middle. Today's dip is far nicer, and I encountered it at one of my favourite fish restaurants, the Green Street Seafood Café in Bath (phone number 01225 448707 – it also has branches in Christchurch, Dorset and Bristol). They serve it with a selection of breads, but the one that went best was a soft-crusted ciabatta.

NO COOKING: *ready in 10 minutes, make shortly before eating*

MAKES 300ml/^{1}/$_2$ PINT

1 large garlic clove	juice of 1 large lemon
a handful of mixed fresh herbs,	175 ml/6 fl oz extra-virgin olive oil
including parsley, mint and basil	salt and plenty of pepper
2 anchovies from a tin, drained	1 tbsp capers (optional)
and rinsed	1 tbsp pine kernels, toasted

❶ Process the garlic till chopped finely, then add the herbs and anchovies and chop fairly finely. With the machine running, pour in the lemon juice, then the oil and seasoning (check the salt because of the anchovies, and the capers, if using). It will form a beautiful green emulsion.

❷ Stir in drained, rinsed capers, if using, and pour into small bowls for dipping. Sprinkle decoratively with pine kernels as a finishing touch.

T I P When using a processor to deal with several different ingredients, always put the one you want most chopped finely in first, and chunkiest at the end. No one wants great lumps of garlic floating round in a finished dish, so I always make sure this is completely pulverised before adding the other ingredients.

PRAWN AND MASCARPONE RAMEKINS

This is a brilliant dinner party starter invented by **Daily Express** *reader Pat Bradshaw of Rochdale, whose family urged her to send it in to share in to the newspaper to share with other readers. (Pat's family have christened the dish 'That Fishy Mascarpone Thing' but it is in fact a rich and delicate little dish!) It is specially convenient for entertaining because you can make it the day before and keep it in the fridge. Serve with salad and, if you wish, triangles of brown bread and butter.*

NO COOKING: *allow 30 minutes to make, at least 4 hours in the fridge*

SERVES 4

250 g tub of mascarpone
125 g/4 oz dolcelatte cheese
16 large cooked and peeled
    prawns

125 g/4 oz smoked salmon or
    smoked trout, chopped up
4 sprigs of fresh parsley, to decorate
slices of lemon, to serve

❶ Mix the mascarpone and dolcelatte together. Line four small ramekins (about 125 ml/4 fl oz each) with cling film and arrange 4 prawns in each, with a sprig of parsley.

❷ Add a layer using half of the mascarpone mixture, then a layer using all of the fish, then the remaining mascarpone. Fold over the cling film and chill for at least 4 hours.

❸ Turn out to serve, and accompany with lemon.

TIPS 🥣 You can use any prawns of your fancy for this recipe, though obviously they need to be shelled.
You can add the sprig of parsley after turning out, if you prefer.

RASPBERRY SYLLABUB ETON MESS

Eton Mess, like the Eton Boating Song, is a something of a school tradition and, though the original is simply strawberries, meringues and whipped cream stirred together, many variations are possible.

EASY: *allow 15 minutes – make no more than 1–2 hours ahead*

SERVES 4

3 ready-made meringues

375 g/12 oz fresh raspberries

4 tbsp dry white wine

75 g/3 oz caster sugar

finely grated zest and juice of
   1 lemon

284 ml carton of double cream

icing sugar, for dusting

❶ Break the meringues into bite-sized pieces into a bowl and add 275 g/ 9 oz of the raspberries.

❷ In a large bowl, stir together the wine, sugar, lemon zest and juice, until the sugar has dissolved. Using a wire whisk, gradually whisk in the cream. Keep whisking until the cream just holds its shape (see Tip).

❸ Spoon the syllabub over the meringue and raspberries and gently stir everything together. Take care not to overmix or the cream will turn pink. Spoon the mixture into a serving bowl, scatter with the remaining raspberries and chill until it's time to serve. Dust with icing sugar just before serving.

TIP 🥣 You could use an electric hand whisk to make the syllabub, but don't over-whisk the cream or it will become too stiff to mix with the meringue and raspberries.

---

no cooking required

SMOKED CHICKEN SALAD

If you can find smoked chicken – from good delicatessens – this is the perfect dish to show it to advantage. Pretty colours and good flavours make it perfect for a summer lunch.

NO COOKING: *20 minutes to assemble*

SERVES 4 – 6

1 smoked chicken or 500 g/1 lb	For the dressing:
skinned, boned, cooked chicken	a small tub of plain thick yogurt
2 celery sticks	4 tbsp olive oil
1 lettuce	4 tbsp orange juice
50 g pack of roasted, salted peanuts	1 tsp paprika
2 oranges	a dash of Tabasco sauce (optional)
a handful of fresh herbs	a pinch of sugar
	salt and pepper

❶ Skin and shred the flesh of the smoked chicken or shred the chicken. Slice the celery and lettuce and put in a bowl, with the peanuts. Refrigerate if you go thus far in advance.

❷ Whisk the dressing ingredients with salt and pepper.

❸ Just before serving, peel and slice the oranges thinly and chop the herbs. Toss all together and serve.

TIP 🥄 Tabasco, or 'liquid fire' as it is sometimes known, is the cleverest seasoning ever – capable of perking up almost any dish either before or during cooking, or sprinkled on (judiciously) when serving.

CHERRY TOMATOES WITH SMOKED SALMON

This simple dish is good for a lunch or dinner-party starter, or as a nibble for a drinks party. The recipe is based on a wonderful canapé I ate on a rather privileged visit to the American Ambassador's residence in London's Regent's Park; the appetisers served with drinks were so irresistible I needed no dinner that evening.

NO COOKING: *allow 30 minutes to make*

SERVES 4 AS A STARTER

2 × 250 g packets of cherry tomatoes (see Tips)

3 spring onions

200 g/7 oz smoked salmon

juice of 1 lemon

1 tbsp olive oil

a few fresh chives

salt and pepper

❶ Wash and dry the tomatoes. Cut a slice off the top, then carefully scoop out the flesh with a teaspoon (see Tips). Peel and chop the onions really finely and dice the salmon very small. Put the onions and salmon in a bowl, with the lemon juice, oil and seasoning. Mix well. Snip the chives on to a plate.

❷ Stuff the tomatoes with the salmon mixture and pop a few chives on top. If serving as a starter, accompany with toast.

TIPS ⬭ If you are lucky enough to find them, use half yellow cherry tomatoes, half red.

It seems a shame to chuck away the tomato flesh in step 1, though it doesn't amount to very much at the end of the day. Either add to a summer soup if making or, if you are very diligent, freeze and add next time you're making stock.

COUNTRY HAM PÂTÉ

The success of this recipe really depends on the quality of ham. Look carefully at the different types and, at the deli, ask for a taste – you will be surprised by your own skill as a taster, because different types taste dramatically different and you will soon isolate your favourite. I think it is a pity in this country that we don't generally taste foods before purchase (something which is obligatory in France) because it is a way to train your tastebuds, and of course keeps your supplier on his toes.

NO COOKING: *allow 15 minutes to make*

MAKES 4–6 RAMEKINS – OR MORE AS A NIBBLE (SEE TIP)

125 g/4 oz best-quality ham, sliced thinly

50 g/2 oz unsalted butter, at room temperature

2 tbsp cream cheese

freshly ground black pepper

❶ Set aside 25 g/1 oz of the ham, and chop the rest coarsely. Process finely, then add the butter, cream cheese and plenty of pepper.

❷ Slice the remaining ham neatly into matchsticks. Add this to the mixture and process with the pulse button just once or twice, to blend – do not overmix.

❸ Put into small ramekins and serve chilled with toast as a first course. Alternatively, chill then spread on biscuits as an appetiser.

T I P 🥣 The idea of 'potting' meat or fish into ramekins with butter and seasoning is an old one. Potted shrimps have survived as a favourite to this day, but it is also a brilliant way to use up leftover game or duck (or at Christmas, goose) and make it go a little further than it otherwise might. The secret is to use plenty of butter and seasoning (though in this recipe this is also supplied by the ham) and to chill before serving.

HAM AND PRAWN CORNETS

*Over the past decade, recipe-writers, led by the restaurant world, have
encouraged home cooks to be free and easy in terms of presentation.
My theory is that restaurant-goers rebelled against the contrived style
of nouvelle cuisine – in which the food was required literally to make
a picture on the plate. So, when I came across this vintage recipe for
a no-cook starter, which doesn't at all follow today's relaxed 'rules'
on presentation, I couldn't resist whipping it up for nostalgia's sake.
I hope you will give it a try too, because (slightly updated) it is
delicious and looks (in a rather retro way) beautiful.*

NO COOKING: *takes a pleasant 40 minutes to put together; can be
made in advance*

SERVES 6

2 tbsp mayonnaise, such as
   Hellmann's

1 tsp tomato ketchup

1 tsp Tabasco sauce

grated zest and juice of 1 orange

2 spring onions, chopped finely

6 sprigs of fresh coriander, chopped

150 g/5 oz small prawns, shelled

3 medium heads of chicory, washed
   and divided into leaves

6 thin slices of good cooked ham

a handful of rocket or watercress

salt and pepper

❶ Mix the mayo, ketchup, Tabasco, salt and pepper in a bowl. Add the
zest of the orange and 1 tbsp of the juice.

❷ Add the spring onions, coriander and prawns. Set aside the 6 best
chicory leaves and chop the rest – stir into the salad.

❸ Lay out a slice of ham on a plate, spread the mixture down the
middle and roll into a cornet.

❹ Remove to a serving plate or individual plates and garnish with the
remaining chicory and watercress or rocket.

WHIPPED RICOTTA WITH BERRIES

This dessert is a bit of a trick: you whip low fat and cream cheese together and leave them to set into a sort of thick mousse that your guests will think you have taken considerable trouble to make.

If you haven't used ricotta in your cooking, it is a light Italian soft cheese, rather like a smooth curd or cottage cheese. It does have a delicate flavour of its own, though, and a lovely texture.

DELICIOUSLY INVENTIVE: *allow half an hour plus 2 hours in the fridge*

SERVES 6, EASILY HALVED

2 × 250 g tubs or packs of ricotta cheese

100 g tub or pack of Philadelphia cream cheese

4 tbsp golden caster sugar

3 tbsp honey

½ tsp vanilla extract

675 g/1½ lb autumn berries – such as blackberries, late strawberries (or whatever is in the shops)

juice of ½ lemon

golden icing sugar, sifted, to serve

❶ Blend the ricotta, cream cheese, half the sugar, honey and vanilla in a processor till completely smooth. Transfer to a serving dish. Cover the bowl and refrigerate till lightly set, about 2 hours, or make a day ahead if you prefer.

❷ Lightly toss together the fruit, lemon juice and remaining caster sugar and let stand for up to half an hour to macerate.

❸ Spoon the cream mixture into wine glasses and top with the fruit. Dust with a little icing sugar to serve.

TIPS 🥣 The ricotta you buy in tubs is different from the type you can buy loose in Italian shops and cheese shops. The sort in the tubs is more grainy and coarse in texture; the fresh sort from a cheesemonger smooth and silky. Obviously the latter is nicer, with a fresher tang, but if you process it well in step 1, you will hardly notice the difference in this recipe.

---

no cooking required

chapter 10

SPECIAL OCCASIONS

All good cooks have a few favourite tricks up their sleeves to bring out on high days and holidays. In this chapter you'll find a few of mine: my favourite Christmas cake and pud recipes, the brandy butter to go with them, the sauce that makes my barbecues the tangiest in town, and treats to add a special touch to your entertaining.

DEVILLED NUTS: WARM SPICED RUM WALNUTS

Essential for a drinks party

EASY: *take 10 minutes to prepare and 12 minutes to cook*

SERVES 6

250 g/8 oz walnut halves

For the spice mix:

2 tbsp caster sugar

¾ tsp crushed sea salt

½ tsp ground cinnamon

a good pinch each of ground cloves and allspice

For the glaze:

1 tbsp rum

2 tsp vanilla extract

1 tsp brown sugar

1 tbsp butter

❶ Toast the walnuts for 8 minutes on a baking sheet lined with baking parchment in an oven preheated to 180°C/160°C fan oven/Gas Mark 4. Put the spices in a bowl. Bring the glaze ingredients to a simmer in a pan.

❷ Tip the walnuts into the glaze and boil for 2 minutes, stirring and shaking all the time, till liquid has evaporated. Tip into the spice mix, toss well and return to baking parchment to cool.

DEVILLED NUTS: MEXICAN ALMONDS

Sweet and spicy at the same time. Serve these nuts in small bowls. I am no fan of Tequila although this would be an authentic accompaniment.
EASY: *take 10 minutes to prepare and 12 minutes to cook.*

SERVES 6

125 g/4 oz flaked almonds
75 g/3 oz roasted peanuts
 (not salted)
25 g/1 oz pumpkin seeds
For the spice mix:
1 tbsp sugar
1 tsp crushed sea salt

½ tsp each of ground cinnamon,
 cumin and coriander
a good pinch of cayenne
For the glaze:
2 tbsp water
1 tsp brown sugar
1 tbsp butter

❶ Toast the almonds on a baking sheet lined with baking parchment in a oven preheated to 180°C/160°C fan oven/Gas Mark 4 for 4 minutes. Add the peanuts and pumpkin seeds and toast for 4 minutes longer. Put the spices in a bowl. Bring the glaze ingredients to a simmer in a pan.

❷ Tip the almonds, peanuts and pumpkin seeds into the glaze and boil for 2 minutes, stirring and shaking all the time, till liquid has evaporated. Tip into the spice mix, toss well and return to baking parchment to cool.

DEVILLED NUTS: INDIAN CASHEWS AND PISTACHIOS

My favourite on the snack front: an exciting sweet and sour mix.
EASY?: *10 minutes to prepare and 12 minutes to cook.*

SERVES 6

175 g/6 oz cashew nuts
50 g/2 oz unsalted shelled
  pistachios
2 tbsp currants
For the spice mix:
1 tbsp sugar
1 tsp salt

1 tsp curry powder
¼ tsp each ground cumin and
  coriander
For the glaze:
2 tbsp water
1 tsp sugar
1 tbsp butter

❶ Toast the cashews for 8 minutes on a baking sheet lined with baking parchment in an oven preheated to 180°C/160°C fan oven/Gas Mark 4. Put the spices in a bowl. Bring the glaze ingredients to a simmer in a pan. Add the pistachios to the baking sheet and toast on for 2 minutes. Mix with the currants.

❷ Tip the cashews and pistachios into the glaze and boil for 2 minutes, stirring and shaking all the time, till liquid has evaporated. Tip into the spice mix, toss well and return to baking parchment to cool.

HOME-MADE APRICOT JAM

I made the recipe several times to experiment with the microwave method – which works a treat – and also with organic and non-organic dried apricots. Although the resulting jam is much darker, organic apricots give a far better flavour, and cook to a much greater tenderness, and I recommend them. You will find them in health shops or the organic sections of supermarkets, and be warned, they do look rather dingy till you taste them.

VERY EASY: *10 minutes to prepare, 10–30 minutes to cook, depending on method*

MAKES 550 g / 1 lb 2 oz

250 g pack of dried apricots

150 g/5 oz caster sugar

juice of ½ lemon

TO MAKE IN THE MICROWAVE

This method works perfectly and the jam is better than made any other way.

❶ Cut the apricots into thin strips. Put in a 2-litre/3½-pint glass bowl or microwaveable casserole with 300 ml/½ pint of water, cover loosely with cling film and microwave on high for 5 minutes.

❷ Stir in the lemon juice and sugar and microwave on high for a further 9 minutes, stirring after 3 minutes. It is done when no sugar crystals remain and the jam appears softly set. Remove from microwave and stir immediately to stop the jam continuing to cook. Ladle into hot clean jars, seal, cool and keep in the fridge for up to a month.

TO MAKE ON THE HOB

❶ Cut the apricots into strips and simmer with 450 ml/¾ pint of water for 30 minutes, till tender.

❷ Add the sugar and lemon juice and cook on for about 10 minutes, until the jam sets when a little is put on a chilled saucer. Ladle into hot clean jars, seal, cool and keep in the fridge for up to a month.

HOME-MADE MUESLI

This recipe is for when you find you've lots of ends of packets left in the larder, and want to use up fruits and nuts before they pass their date. EASY: *allow 30 minutes; keeps well for a fortnight in a plastic box*

MAKES 2 kg/4 1/2 lb CEREAL

875 g/1¾ lb jumbo or rolled (porridge) oats
100 ml/4 fl oz runny honey, mixed with 2 tbsp oil
750 g/1½ lb mixed nuts, whole or chopped as you prefer
500 g/1 lb dried fruits – including dried peaches, organic dried apricots and so on

❶ If you don't fancy washing up your roasting tin after cooking, line with extra-wide turkey foil. Otherwise, grease well. Preheat the oven to 190°C/170°C fan oven/Gas Mark 5.

❷ Put the oats in the lined tin. Mix the honey and oil to a strange Swarfega-like consistency and pour over the oats. Bake for 10 minutes or so, stirring a couple of times, till beginning to toast, then add the nuts and toast on for a further 10 minutes till all is pale golden. Keep an eye on it and stir whenever you remember.

❸ Leave to cool and, when cold, mix in the fruit.

T I P This is so full of good things you may wish to dilute it a bit with porridge oats or toasted porridge oats.

TUTTI FRUTTI BRANDY BUTTER

Brandy butter is extremely easy to make, and invariably nicer than the shop-bought versions. My recipe is two-recipes-in-one: I make a delicious marinated fruit mixture, (great for ice cream or in a bread and butter pud) and then use some of that to add colour and panache to the brandy butter.

MIRABELLE GLACÉ FRUITS IN BRANDY: *Makes about 275 g/9 oz: keeps up to 2 months in fridge*

❶ Chop 50 g/2 oz each of peel, glacé ginger and sultanas. For a more colourful effect, add glacé cherries, pineapple or angelica. Put in a small jar, cover with 8–10 tbsp brandy and shake well.

MIRABELLE BRANDY BUTTER: *Makes about 250 g/8 oz – enough to serve 10–14: freezes well*

According to Constance Spry, brandy butter is also known as 'Senior Wrangler Sauce'. A Senior Wrangler is a Cambridge term to describe an academic with the top degree in mathematics. I suspect therefore that, like crème brûlée, this sauce found favour in the august dining hall of some Cambridge college.

❶ Cream 75 g/3 oz of softened unsalted butter with 75 g/3 oz of icing or caster sugar. Beat in 3 tbsp of brandy and 3 tbsp of Mirabelle Glacé Fruits. Chill or freeze. The most satisfactory way I know of serving brandy butter is to cut in neatish portion-size cubes while frozen and pile in a shallow dish. Mathematicians will probably wish to cut 14 cubes and pile them into a perfect pyramid. Serve chilled or at room temperature as you prefer.

T I P Icing sugar gives a smoother effect, caster a more grainy effect. If you can get it, Billington's Muscovado Icing Sugar has a far better flavour than the white stuff.

LIGHT CHRISTMAS PUDDING

This is a light and fragrant version of the Christmas pudding and, although the long boiling makes it nice and dark, it is not the solid fruit and spice affair of Victorian origin.

WORTH THE TROUBLE: *allow a morning or afternoon; keep in fridge or freeze*

MAKES ONE 1.75-LITRE/3-PINT PUDDING OR TWO OR THREE SMALLER ONES

500 g/1 lb raisins	**½ tsp ground cloves**
300 g/10 oz currants	**250 g/8 oz chilled butter, chopped**
475 ml/16 fl oz water	**4 large eggs**
125 g/4 oz fine white breadcrumbs	**100 ml/3½ fl oz brandy**
75 g/3 oz plain flour	**100 ml/3½ fl oz sweet sherry, port**
175 g/6 oz dark muscovado sugar	**or marsala**
1 tsp salt	**50 g/2 oz cut mixed peel**
2 tsp ground cinnamon	**extra brandy, for flaming the**
2 tsp ground ginger	**pudding**

❶ Simmer the raisins and currants in the water for 12–15 minutes, till the water has evaporated. Leave to cool – about an hour.

❷ Whizz the breadcrumbs, flour, sugar, salt and spices in a processor. Add the butter and process carefully until it forms a crumbly mixture – do not carry on until the mixture binds. Transfer to a bowl; no need to wash up the processor bowl. In the processor bowl, process the eggs till foamy, add the brandy and sherry then stir into the breadcrumb mixture with a whisk. Add the peel and cooled raisins and currants. Get the family to stir and make a wish.

❸ Thickly butter one 1.75-litre/3-pint or two 900 ml/1½-pint basins (or other combinations as you wish). Spoon in mixture to fill basins to within 2 cm/¾ inch of the top. Make a lid of foil and crimp tightly round the edges, then tie tightly with string. Cut off any overhang.

4 Set a trivet or trivets in boiling water, add pudding or puddings and boil, covered, for 2½ hours (small size) to 3½ hours (large size), keeping the water boiling very fast for the first half hour.

5 The puddings can be stored either left in the original basin and wrapped with clean foil or turned out, if you need the basin. If turning out, do so while the pudding is still hot and wrap well in two sheets of foil. Once cool, puddings are best refrigerated and will keep for up to two months.

6 On the day, return unmoulded pudding to a well buttered mould if necessary and boil for 1½ hours. Turn out, flame with warmed brandy and serve with Tutti Frutti Brandy Butter (page 197).

T I P I tie extra loops of string round the basin to make a handle for lifting out when step 3 has finished. Unless you are using a comfortable-size pan it can be very hard to get your oven-mitted hands in to lift out the pud.

SAUSAGE AND WALNUT STUFFING

This is a simple but extremely tasty stuffing that will perfectly complement the festive bird without making too much of a statement. At times like Christmas, traditions are to be honoured, and I don't go for such newfangled additions as dried cranberries.

EASY: *30 minutes to make, 35 minutes to cook on the day; freezes well or make up to 2 days before eating*

SERVES 10–12

500 g/1 lb best sausagemeat

50 g/2 oz butter

3 onions, chopped

2 celery sticks, chopped

2 tsp salt

½ tsp ground black pepper

375 g/12 oz fresh breadcrumbs, white, brown or wholemeal

2 tbsp chopped fresh herbs, or 2 tsp dried

125 g/4 oz raisins or sultanas

125 g/4 oz chopped walnuts or pecans

425 ml/¾ pint stock and extra butter (see step 3)

❶ Brown the sausagemeat for 8 minutes in a large pan. No fat is necessary, but break up meat with a spatula as it cooks. Remove with a slotted spoon to a large bowl. Add the butter and fry the chopped vegetables for 10 minutes over a moderate heat, until lightly golden.

❷ Add to the sausagement with the seasoning, breadcrumbs, herbs, raisins or sultanas and nuts. Chill.

❸ If intending to stuff the bird, use as the stuffing as it is. If intending to bake separately, mix in the stock and a little extra melted butter, then pack into a small buttered tin. Bake at 180°C/160°C fan oven/Gas Mark 4, covered, for 15 minutes, then for a further 20 minutes uncovered.

TIP This stuffing will be as good as the sausagemeat you start with, so buy the best you can find and, if possible, experiment in advance.

SLOW-ROASTED TOMATOES

This is delicious and clever ingredient to make for your storecupboard to use in place of sun-dried tomatoes; they are much tenderer and nicer flavoured.

WORTH THE TROUBLE: *40 minutes to prepare, 3 hours to cook; keeps for a fortnight in the fridge*

MAKES 1 MEDIUM-SIZE JAR

10 large ripe beefsteak tomatoes	**sea salt**
(about 250 g/8 oz each)	**125 ml/4 fl oz olive oil**

❶ Preheat the oven to 150°C/130°C fan oven/Gas Mark ½. Line a large, deep baking tray or roasting tin with baking parchment. Boil a kettle and get a large bowl of cold water ready.

❷ First, skin the tomatoes. Do this by cutting out the tough white core and slashing the other end with a cross. Put 3–4 tomatoes in a bowl and pour boiling water over them. After 20–30 seconds transfer to the bowl of cold water, then, one by one, peel off the skins. Repeat till all are skinned.

❸ Now prepare the tomatoes. This takes about half an hour, so you might as well put on the radio and enjoy yourself. Quarter each one, then scrape away all the seeds and cut out the interior ribs and flesh so you are left with just the outside flesh, which should be a quarter-moon shape. Repeat with all the tomatoes, laying overlapping fashion, rather like roof tiles, in the roasting tin. Drizzle thoroughly with the oil, sprinkle generously with salt and put in the oven.

❹ Roast for 2½–3 hours, reducing the heat if they start to blacken at the edges. They will have shrunk to about half the size, deepened in colour and be firm, if slippery, to the touch. Put in a jar – a 500 g/1 lb jamjar should suffice – and cover with fresh oil.

SWEET AND TANGY
BBQ SAUCE

This recipe is my all-time-favourite barbecue marinade.

A RECIPE FOR THE PERFECTIONIST: *allow 40 minutes; keeps for a week or freezes well*

MAKES ABOUT 400ml/14floz

1 onion, quartered

275 ml/9 fl oz ketchup

2 tbsp cider vinegar

2 tbsp Worcestershire sauce

2 tbsp Dijon mustard

5 tbsp black treacle

1 tsp Tabasco sauce

¼ tsp ground black pepper

2 tbsp vegetable oil

1 medium garlic clove, crushed

1 tsp chilli powder

¼ tsp cayenne pepper

❶ Process the onion with 75 ml/2½ fl oz of water in a food processor for 30 seconds or till slushy. Strain into a small bowl.

❷ Whisk in the ketchup, vinegar, Worcestershire sauce, mustard, treacle, Tabasco and pepper.

❸ Heat the oil in a large pan until good and hot. Add the garlic, chilli powder and cayenne pepper and cook until fragrant – about 30 seconds. Whisk in the ketchup mixture and bring to a boil, then simmer, uncovered, for about 25 minutes. Cool and use as a marinade and dressing for all barbecued foods.

TIP If you manage to find an odd-sounding American flavouring called 'liquid smoke', add 1½ tsp at step 2.

VALENTINE CREAM LIQUEUR

Cream liqueurs are all the rage. My favourite must be Sheridan's, which delivers itself into the glass in a beautiful brown and white striped pattern. My recipe, which was created for Valentine's Day, is flavoured with chocolate, whisky, vanilla and coffee – the ultimate after-dinner combo.

You can drink this neat, or on the rocks, and, if there is some left (it will keep for a fortnight in the refrigerator), it is great poured over ice cream.

NO COOKING: *10 minutes plus 2 hours chilling*

SERVES 8

397 ml can of sweetened
  condensed milk

250 ml/8 fl oz whisky

1 tbsp chocolate syrup or chocolate
  sauce (in jars – see Tips)

1 tbsp vanilla extract or ½ tsp
  vanilla essence

1 tsp instant coffee powder or
  granules

250 ml/8 fl oz whipping cream

❶ Combine the first 5 ingredients in a blender and blend until the coffee dissolves – about a minute.

❷ Add the whipping cream and blend for a further 10 seconds.

❸ Transfer to jug and chill for a couple of hours. If you really can't wait, pour over ice and serve immediately.

TIPS 🥣 Do check your condensed milk is sweetened (not to be confused with evaporated milk, which is not, or condensed unsweetened, which is also available).

You can get various different chocolate sauces in the supermarket, designed to be poured over ice cream. Try to get a dark-chocolate rather than a milk-chocolate one.

CHOCOLATE TRUFFLES

This is a recipe for the perfectionist. Though not much cheaper than bought truffles, these are out of all comparison for flavour and texture. They would make a brilliant gift, if you can bear to give them away. Allow 2 hours from start to finish; keeps for a week in the fridge

MAKES ABOUT 150g/5oz (18–24 TRUFFLES, DEPENDING ON SIZE), QUANTITIES EASILY DOUBLED

For the filling:

125 g/4 oz best dark chocolate

50 ml/2 fl oz double cream

15 g/½ oz unsalted butter

2 tsp maple syrup or liquid glucose

1 tbsp brandy, rum or liqueur
 (mint liqueur is good)

For the coating:

125 g/4 oz best dark chocolate

75 g/3 oz cocoa powder (not
 drinking chocolate)

❶ Make the centres. Melt the chocolate in the microwave or in a bowl over simmering water. In a small pan, bring the cream, butter and syrup to a simmer. Remove from the heat and set aside for 5 minutes.

❷ Whisk the cooled cream mixture into the chocolate until smooth. Whisk in the alcohol. Cool to room temperature – 45 minutes.

❸ Whisk the chocolate mixture for just 30 seconds – no longer or it will spoil the texture. Scrape into a pastry bag fitted with a 1 cm/½-inch plain nozzle and pipe small round blobs or mini-logs on to a baking sheet lined with baking parchment; alternatively put into a plastic bag and snip off corner and use as piping bag, or use a melon baller or just a teaspoon. Refrigerate till firm – about half an hour.

❹ To coat the truffles, melt the remaining chocolate in a wide bowl or pan and allow to cool to blood heat. Sift the cocoa into a swiss roll tin; have ready a plastic sieve and arm yourself with a fork. Though it sounds messy, use your left hand to dip each truffle into the chocolate, rolling in your palm to coat all over. Drop into the cocoa and using the fork in your right hand (keep this hand chocolate free!), roll the truffle round in the cocoa to coat. Leave for 2 minutes to firm up then transfer with the fork to the sieve; roll round over the swiss roll tin to remove excess cocoa. The truffles are now finished. Keep in an airtight container in the fridge and eat within a week.

T I P S 🥣 If you have surgical gloves, you can spare yourself the messiness of handling the chocolate.

To get the the last smidgin of chocolate out of the piping bag, press out with one of those flat pastry scrapers.

INDEX

i n d e x